AMAZING ANIMALS

Meet the Cleverest, Cutest, and Most Incredible Animals on the Planet!

Adam Phillips

BARRON'S

Quotation sources:
12 Safari park spokesman to the UK's *Daily Mail* newspaper; **15** Anthropologist David Daegling from Wikipedia; **19** Posting from YouTube viewer; **22** Photographer Michael Hutchinson from Getty Images caption; **26** Photographer Eric Cheng to the UK's *Daily Telegraph* newspaper; **31** Farmer Linsber Brister to *The Ledger* newspaper, Lakeland, Florida; **34** Researcher Chris Bird from Rex Features story; **36** Deaf dog trainer Liz Grewal from Rex Features story; **41** Amateur photographer Charles Lam from Rex Features story; **43** Safari park trainer Dinah Wilson to Fox News in the USA; **45** Pet wigmaker Crissy Slaughter from Rex Features story; **48** Photographer Paul Hughes from Barcroft Media; **52** Wildlife photographer Kathleen Reeder from Rex Features story; **55** Monkey owner Tommy Lucia to the *Denver Post* newspaper, USA; **57** Homeowner Chris Marin to the Associated Press; **61** Conservation-grazing warden Carol Laidlow at Wicken Fen from Rex Features story; **62** Photographer Geoff Robinson from Rex Features story; **64** Lion expert Kevin Richardson to the UK's *Daily Mail* newspaper; **71** Chief snake charmer Babanath Mithunath Madari to the UK's *Daily Mail* newspaper; **75** Dog class dance teacher Mayumi Ozuma to Reuters; **77** Pigeon hotel owner Mary Bartlett from Rex Features story; **78** Animal photographer Ren Netherland to *Pet Industry* magazine; **80** Cheetah owner Riana Van Nieuwenhuizen to the UK's *Daily Mail* newspaper; **83** Owner of the Sriracha Crocodile Farm, Arporn Samakit, to Lanka Business Online; **89** Bird scientist Dr Allan Baker to *National Geographic* magazine; **90** Dr William Wallace from the Buena Pet Clinic quoted on Giant George, the world's tallest dog website; **94** Naturalist Sir David Attenborough

Picture credits:
Front cover: Bronek Kaminski/Barcroft Media Ltd.
Back cover (tl) UPPA/Photoshot, (tr) REUTERS/Osman Orsal, (bl) Tom Farmer/Rex Features , (br) REUTERS/Str Old

Disclaimer: Every effort has been made to locate the sources of the images reproduced within.
Should the copyright holder wish to contact the publisher, please write to Arcturus Publishing in London.

First edition for North America published in 2011
by Barron's Educational Series, Inc.

Copyright © 2011, Arcturus Publishing Limited

First published in 2010 by Arcturus Publishing Limited
26/27 Bickels Yard, 151-153 Bermondsey Street
London SE1 3HA

Author: Adam Phillips
In-house editor: Kate Overy

All inquiries should be addressed to:
Barron's Educational Series, Inc.
250 Wireless Boulevard
Hauppauge, New York 11788
www.barronseduc.com

ISBN-13: 978-0-7641-4679-4
ISBN-10: 0-7641-4679-3

Library of Congress Catalog Card. No.: 2010934143

Manufactured by NPE, Kallang, Singapore
November 2010

9 8 7 6 5 4 3 2 1

Contents

Introduction	page 5
Born Free-ky	page 6
Strictly Animal	page 18
Clever Creatures	page 32
Pet Pastimes	page 42
Incredible Tales	page 54
Animal Obsessed	page 70
Crazy Critters	page 82
Index & Credits	page 96

MONKEY RODEO
Check out this superstar on page 55!

4

Introduction

In this book, we've scoured the planet to find the craziest creatures, the most record-breaking beasts, and the wildest animal antics in the world. By the time you've finished reading, we can guarantee you won't view wildlife, or even your humble pet, in the same way ever again. So dive in and take a look!

Star Entry

Keep an eye out for our star entries. These are awarded to those beasties that bowled us over the most when putting together this book, like Cedo, the monkey farmer (page 31). These crazy animals left us laughing, in awe, or running off to hide very, very quickly! Believe us, it was difficult choosing just one per chapter.

STAR ENTRY

Better Safe Than Sorry

If you own a pet, remember that your special friend may not be up to taking a plunge in the nearest swimming pool or free-falling from a great height while strapped to your chest. So always exercise caution when handling animals and remember to accept your beloved pet for what it is – a brilliant companion, friend, and playmate!

CHAPTER 1
Born Free-ky

We know that animals come in all shapes and sizes, but you won't have seen anything quite like the critters featured here! Unique and utterly brilliant, they're proof that Mother Nature is always ready to surprise us.

Look out for...

ZANY HORSE

WHITE CROC

PINT-SIZED PIG

From Puppy with Love

Meet the dog who wears his heart on his sleeve, well, his coat actually. Born in Japan in 2007, this cute Chihuahua belongs to Emiko Sakurada. Out of the 1,000 dogs Emiko bred, he was the first to have such an adorable marking. But he certainly was not the last. Two years later, Heart-kun's brother was born bearing exactly the same mark. He was called Love-kun. Then Love-kun had a son, Kokoro-chan, who also sported the amazing heart shape on his coat. We think this could be the start of a new Japanese dynasty. But if you're thinking of buying one of these super-cute dogs, then stop right now. Emiko has said she will never, ever sell her adorable Chihuahuas.

The White Stuff

It's not easy being one of only 12 almost pure white alligators in the U.S. when you've got five million gray mates. This fearsome-looking reptile may look scary to us mere humans with that amazing skin and those crazy blue eyes, but out in the wild, he'd be spotted a mile away by predators and prey.

That's why 22-year-old Bouya Blan, pictured here with his handler Tim Williams, was rescued along with some chums from the wild before they all croc-ked it. They're now safe and sound at Gatorland in Florida, enjoying a life of luxury. Each one has its own pool and decking to lounge about on.

What Am I?

Sorry, but we really don't know! This nocturnal creature has been living in Chunati Zoo in China for the last nine years, yet no one has a clue what she is. Despite visits from zoologists, scientists, curious tourists and other people, everyone is bemused by what they are looking at.

She has a pig-like mouth, rabbit-like ears, and a fox-like body, but put them all together and everyone draws a blank. Perhaps the mysterious mammal's most intriguing feature is her eyes, which can change from pink to yellow to ivory-white. It's enough to give anyone a fright if they saw that at night!

THE NAMING GAME

This peculiar new animal species desperately needs a name. Here are a few of our suggestions for the "pig-rabbit-fox." Your turn!

Fox-trotter
Fabbit
Pox
Rab-pig
Robox

The Lizard King(s)

Meet the most doted-on two-headed lizard in the world. According to Californian owners Barbara and Frank Witte, they don't like the two-headed reference; the couple believe that their extraordinary bearded dragon lizard is actually two lizards in one body. To prove it, they have named each head – the one on the right is Zak and on the left is Wheezie.

The pair of U.S. lizards are also famous for being the longest-living of their kind on record and have become celebrities across the world. They even receive birthday cards. When they were younger, Zak and Wheezie attracted so much interest that the Wittes decided to lie low and stay out of the public eye. They were worried about drawing too much unwanted attention from circus sideshow folk!

Twice the Fright ...

... and twice the bite. Not that it would hurt – this two-headed garter snake isn't poisonous, thankfully. Owners of two-headed snakes have discovered that their hotheads fight over food, with the left head always winning. The snakes also have problems deciding which way to go, as one head pulls in one direction and the other in the opposite one. It must all end in a hissy fit!

Painted Pecking

It looks like a controversial practice to most of us, but in the Philippines it's perfectly normal to wander through a market in the capital city of Manila and find two- or three-day-old chicks that have been dyed neon-bright colors. They're hugely popular with children, who pester their parents into buying the chicks as pets. And at a mere 8 cents, they're flying off the shelves. No, not literally ...

Four, Three, Then Two

It might sound like a completely qu-ackers story, but did you hear about the duck that was born with four legs instead of two? The world's media went wild when they first saw Stumpy, the incredible four-legged duck found by breeder Nicky Janaway. They splashed his story all over the newspapers.

Stumpy went on to confound medical experts, who thought he wouldn't live long, by growing up into a perfectly healthy adult. Alas, his extra legs didn't fare so well. One accidentally got pulled off when it became stuck in fencing, and the other one simply shriveled up after this photograph was taken!

Dude, Where Are My Stripes?

Well, they're nowhere to be seen on this pure white Bengal tiger called Fareeda. The first of her kind to be born in Africa, this white wonder is incredibly rare. Even her brother and sister, Shahir and Sitarah, who were born at the same time, have normal black stripes. Fareeda is so rare that she is only one of 20 stripe-less tigers left in the world, and her proud owners at the Cango Wildlife Ranch in South Africa have been taking extra-special care of her. Or specifically, her adoptive mother, Lisha the Labrador, has. This caring canine has looked after more than 30 tigers during the last several years. Fareeda's owners hope that once the young tiger is an adult, she can be released into the wild.

ODD ODDS
The experts weren't sure if newly born Fareeda would remain stripe-less into adult life. In fact the odds of Fareeda staying snowy white were 100 to one.

It's a Zorse!

Or if you prefer, a zebroid – that's a cross between a zebra and a horse. Christened Eclyse when she was born in 2007, this amazing animal is the result of her mother, a horse from a German safari park, going on a holiday to Italy and falling head-over-hoof in love with a strapping young zebra. There are other zorses in existence, such as the one made between a Shetland pony and a zebra in 2001. Zorses normally look like horses but are covered in stripes. As you can see here, Eclyse is quite different. She has zebra stripes on her head and rear, but the rest of her body and her legs are completely white.

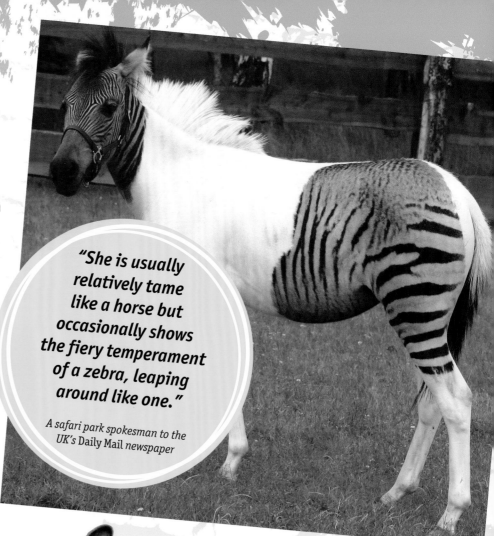

"She is usually relatively tame like a horse but occasionally shows the fiery temperament of a zebra, leaping around like one."

A safari park spokesman to the UK's Daily Mail newspaper

Unicorn Ain't No Myth

Unicorns are supposed to be the stuff of legends, but in 2008, one was found at a nature reserve in Tuscany, Italy. Well, okay, it's actually a young deer named Unicorn who has an incredibly rare single horn on the front of his head. Spoilsport scientists are calling the horn a "genetic mutation." Other, even bigger, spoilsports have suggested that it was perhaps unusual deer such as this one that created the myth of the unicorn in the first place. It's best to ignore the spoilsports, though, by packing your camera and heading off to Tuscany to see if you can get a snap of this notoriously shy superstar.

SPOT THE CELEB
Hundreds of intrigued visitors have descended upon the Italian nature reserve to catch a glimpse of the fabled unicorn deer.

Pint-size Pig

Unlike other pig breeds that start off cute only to grow up big and bad-tempered (much like adult humans), these pint-sized marvels bred on a farm in the United Kingdom stay small and cuddly, and can even be housetrained. For such tiny snouts, the pigs have been a huge hit. Farmer Chris Murray says that he sells 50 a year but has a waiting list of tens of thousands of people all wanting their slice of porky perfection!

Mop Top Is Top Dog

This dog doesn't have time to mop about. Although Fee, the pedigree Hungarian Puli sheepdog, is regularly confused with being a bucket of water's best friend, he also happens to be top dog at pooch shows and is always a clean hit with the crowds.

With his natural "dreadlocked" tresses (known as cords) and expert jumping skills, German owner Eva Meyer reckons that Fee always "wipes the floor with the competition." You might wonder how, with all that hair in front of his eyes. But according to the Puli Club of America, "It's like looking through vertical window blinds, and since the cords move as the Puli does, the view is even better."

HAIR-RAISING!
It took between four and five years to grow Fee's hair this long!

FAMOUS FIENDS

Lock your doors and hide in the cupboard! It's time to meet the world's scariest legendary monsters.

Loch Out, There's a Monster Behind You!

You could never accuse the Loch Ness monster of being shy. It's been spotted by more than 1,000 people in the last 77 years in Scotland's largest freshwater loch, or lake. During that time, descriptions of Nessie have varied wildly – it could have been a prehistoric creature measuring anywhere from 6 ft/1.8 m to 60 ft/18.3 m long, it may have had a long or a short neck and it may or may not have possessed a set of flippers. The monster has been the subject of much investigation since it was first spotted back in the 1930s, from serious scientific research through to fanatics camping out for decades hoping to capture the creature on camera. But still, no one has produced definitive proof that it exists.

NO NESSIE
This startling picture of Nessie poking her head out above the loch's waters was taken in 1934. It was finally revealed to be a hoax in 1994, a whole 60 years later.

El 'Orrible Chupacabra

The legend of El Chupacabra, the dreaded "goat sucker," was born in in Central America during the 1990s when witnesses reported seeing a "demon dog" draining the blood from dead goats like a crazed vampire. Some people believe this creature is a supernatural beast, others that it could even be an escaped monster bred at a U.S. military installation. Skeptical scientists just put it down to a case of a hairless coyote with a bad skin condition!

CREEPY FEATURES

The feared El Chupacabra has been described in so many different ways that you have to wonder what it really looks like! Here are a few of the freakiest:

"It leaps like a kangaroo."

"It has sharp spines growing up its back."

"It has glowing red eyes that can hypnotize its prey."

"It lets off a disgusting eggy smell when alarmed."

Yeti Another Abominable Snowman

From the Himalayan mountains of Nepal and Tibet to areas of California, the Abominable Snowman, also know as the Yeti or Bigfoot, has been spotted at large since the 19th century. Descriptions vary about its scary attributes, but if you see a very tall creature with a pointy head, sporting fur like that of a gorilla and in possession of two enormous feet, you should start running immediately.

There have been numerous sightings over the past 200 years. In 1924, a Yeti reportedly attacked a group of U.S. miners, and in 1953, the legendary climber Sir Edmund Hilary described a set of giant footprints he found in the snow while on a climbing expedition to the top of Mount Everest, in Nepal.

MONKEY MAN

In 1967, American Robert Patterson captured this shot of a Yeti on camera. To this day, people speculate whether it's a distant relative of a bear or ape, or just a man dressed up in a monkey suit!

FEET FIRST

Although people claim to have come face-to-face with the Yeti, most "sightings" are actually of its footprints. This alleged cast of an enormous Yeti footprint is on display at the Beijing Natural History Museum in China.

"Most acquaintances of Patterson volunteered that neither he nor Gimlin were clever enough to put something that detailed together."

Anthropologist David Daegling discussing whether Patterson and his friend Gimlin were playing a prank on the world

Pointy-Eared Cat, It Be

What do a small green alien from the movie series *Star Wars* and a cat from Chicago have in common? Well, they've both got pointy ears, but Yoda the cat has actually got four of them! Although Yoda has to put up with endless bad jokes about being a good listener, he is actually an utterly normal puss. His owners love him so much that they have had a tiny computer chip fitted inside him. Now if he ever goes missing, or is kidnapped by Darth Maul, they can track him across the universe and rescue him!

STAR WARS SUPERSTAR
When Yoda the cat's pictures first appeared online, TV channels went berserk trying to get him on their talk shows. What a star!

World's Tiniest Lamb

Called Mathilde, this little bitty black lamb is the smallest lamb in the world. She was born on a rare-breeds farm in Suffolk, England, and comes from the Ouessant breed of sheep, which is the world's smallest type of sheep. Ouessant sheep originated on one small island off the coast of France. Some people reckon that the wooly wonders are descended from an ancient Viking breed, ideal for storing aboard longships because of their diminutive size.

VERTICAL CHALLENGE
Even when they grow up to be adults, Ouessant sheep stay tiny. Rams reach 19 in/49 cm height to their shoulder and ewes reach 18 in/45 cm.

Spot the Gecko

For such a tiny creature, this scaly-eyed gecko has sure got a long, long name – Lepidoblepharis buschwaldii. This mini gecko, small enough to sit on top of a pencil, was discovered for the first time on a recent scientific expedition to the rain forests of Ecuador.

It wasn't the only new species to be found. His new buddies include a blunt-snouted slug-sucking snake, three species of lungless salamanders that breathe through their skin and 30 species of rain frogs. Perhaps the most freaky amphibian find was a glass frog. Its skin is translucent so you can see all its internal organs. Talk about hopping horrible!

A Very Peculiar Pig

Best rub your eyes and then pinch yourself, then rub your eyes again. This really is a pig and not a bizarre type of sheep with a pig's head! Known as Mangalitza pigs, these crazy animals feature amazing wooly coats that help them survive harsh winters and protect them from sunburn in the summers. Their coats come in three different colors – blonde, black (with a creamy tummy) and bright red. For the bacon lovers among you, the Mangalitza pig is much fattier than a normal pig. Go on, pass the ketchup!

PIGS ON PARADE
The Mangalitza breed of pig became extinct in the United Kingdom in 1972, but thanks to a special breeding program, the porky snorters have been reared in captivity again.

CHAPTER 2
Strictly Animal

Get ready to do a double take as you "paw" your way through this incredible chapter. The animal behavior featured here is strangely human, but it's strictly animal too!

Look out for...

LOLLY-LOVING OTTER

WATERBABE PIG

MONKEY FARMER

Pedal Power Pup

Boredom has always been a bone of contention for super-smart pooch Momotaro. Not happy with being able to walk like a human or even spin Hula Hoops, this Dalmatian is so determined to be like us that he has learned to cycle!

His owner, Kazuhiro Nishi, helped to teach the spotty wannabe cyclist to ride a bike in a mere six weeks. Now a regular sight on the streets of Chiba, just outside Tokyo in Japan, the Dalmatian pants, puffs, and pedals his way along, entertaining the local kids and starring in Japanese TV shows for canine-cycling fans!

"A dog on a bike is fine, but I prefer a cat on a pogo stick."

A posting from a viewer on YouTube proves that you can't please everybody

Cat Burglar

Patience obviously isn't this cat's best character trait. Whenever Charlie makes a beeline to get back into the apartment where he lives, he can't be bothered to wait for someone to open the front door. Instead he climbs 13 ft/4 m to get onto the apartment's balcony – and that's no tall story, it's actually two stories!

Nicknamed Spider-Cat by the locals in Falkirk, Scotland, Charlie uses his front paws to grip the rough wall while his rear paws push up. Experts reckon this mountaineering moggy must have really strong claws. We reckon he simply has a head for heights.

GO FOR IT, CHARLIE!
The two other cats Charlie shares the apartment with prefer using the front door but are always on paw to give Spider-Cat a meow of support.

CAT IN A FLAP

Kitties love climbing, but they're not always so good at getting back down. Check out these top tree-rescue tips.

• Leave an open can of cat food at the bottom. The smell of tasty fish can overcome any fear of heights.

• Find a ladder and lay it against the tree. The curious kitty will come down.

• If all else fails, call the fire department and let the experts sort it out!

Buffalo Wins

Imagine sharing your dinner table with a 1,600 lb/726 kg buffalo. Well, it's something that U.S. farmer Jim Sautner endured for eight years. Buffalo Bailey and owner Jim would make small talk in the kitchen, take a drive in the family convertible car and then crash in front of the TV. We wonder if there were any arguments about which channel to watch.

Lounge Lizard

It's tough being a model. You have to work punishing hours, watch the calories, and fight the need to throw tantrums. But for this two-year-old female iguana, lounging about in front of the cameras comes naturally. Trained by 53-year-old Santisak Dulapitak, she's most happy having a "tail" of a time posing in a deck chair, hanging out in a hammock or strumming scales on her guitar. Santisak has been training animals to appear in TV ads and movies for more than 20 years. If you go to his house in Bangkok, Thailand, you can also meet his fully trained python and flock of multitalented flying foxes!

This lizard is a real lazybones!

Monkey Magic in Moscow

With winter temperatures sinking as low as –22°F/–30°C in Moscow, everyone has to wrap up tight so they don't end up as cold as a brass monkey, and that includes this hardworking primate! Eye-catching and dressed for the part, this marvelous monkey works with street photographers in the city square entertaining the locals and tourists alike with its antics.

"It is rare to see a dominant bull so relaxed, as they are usually on the alert for danger ..."

Nature photographer Michael Hutchinson talks about the behavior of the male seal he captured on camera

Sealed with a Laugh

The life of a seal is a tough one, forever hunting for fish and avoiding hungry predators. But like us, they love to take time out to relax, and have a good yawn and even the odd laugh or two. This gray seal was snapped in Lincolnshire, United Kingdom, as he rolled around chortling while patting his full tummy. Perhaps the finely finned fellow was simply laughing at photographer Michael Hutchinson, who got soaked taking the shot. Or perhaps he was just happy that back in 1914, there were only 500 seals in the United Kingdom but today there are 182,000 of these sea mammals packing Britain's beaches.

A Match Made in Doggie Heaven

We've all heard of dating agencies for people, but in São Paulo, Brazil, there's a very special matchmaking service for pining pooches. Once the lucky lassies have found their puppy love, a wedding service can be arranged, after which the bride (and very well groomed) groom can be booked into the marvelous Pet Love Motel. This is a very special place where honeymooning hounds can spend quality time in the lap of luxury, watching videos, listening to music, and feeling right at home with air conditioning and paw print wallpaper. Sounds like doggie heaven!

Cat Makes a Splash

We all know that after mice, cats hate water the most. Now, if we're honest, it doesn't look like this feline is feeling too fine about going for a dip, but U.S. resident Mary Ellen Schesser has been teaching her cats to swim. Why? Well, because if they fell into her swimming pool by accident, she was worried they wouldn't know what to do! Mary has been tutoring her cats in the art of swimming since 2004. She takes them to water three times a year. Mary is actually one smart owner, as more than 1,000 pets meet a watery end each year in U.S. swimming pools.

KITTY PADDLE
Pictured here is cranky-looking Nymbus, a silver Persian, doing the cat-paddle. She is just one of five cats that Mary Schesser owns who have put their paws to water.

ODD COUPLES

Friendships can blossom between the strangest of people, and with animals they happen between the most unlikely of species. Here we profile some of the most endearing and amazing couples to grace the animal kingdom.

Pooch Pampers Her Piglet

Rejected by her mom, alone and near death . . . It sounds like a tragic story. However, as in a Disney film, Paulinchen, the tiny Vietnamese potbellied piglet, ended up enjoying a happily-ever-after ending. The two-week-old baby was discovered by a German farmer on his property, who whisked her up and swiftly presented her to the farmer's giant Rhodesian ridgeback dog, Katjinga. Rather than viewing the piglet as a bacon sandwich, Katjinga fell in love with her right away. She had also just stopped nursing her own litter of pups so was able to feed the hungry hog with her own milk. The two have become inseparable, and Paulinchen is now a healthy, young, perky pig!

Monkey Love

You'd feel very unhappy if you lost your mom, so you can imagine how sad this three-month-old macaque monkey was when he was found wandering alone and close to death on Neilingding Island in China. Although physically fine once nursed back to health, it was obvious that he was still depressed. That was until a big-hearted pigeon winged her way into his life and they became best friends. The melancholy monkey was soon swinging and grinning again.

Chimp-ion of the World!

Anjana the chimp is the world's most amazing nanny. This five-year-old primate became famous in 2009 when her incredible mothering skills were shown off to the public as she fed a nine-week-old puma cub called Sierra. This wasn't just for show though. Anjana works at The Institute of Greatly Endangered and Rare Species (T.I.G.E.R.S.) Preserve in South Carolina, with her human boss, who taught the chimp everything she knows about bringing up little big cats!

Ready for a walk, dear?

Beast of Friends

These two wild animals, a wiry warthog called Poggles and a rumbling rhino called Tatenda, may look like fierce African creatures, but they're softer-than-cotton buds and the world's most unlikely bosom buddies. They became friends when they lost their parents to poachers and were taken in at the Imire Sarfari Ranch in Zimbabwe. Poggles and Tatenda were allowed full run of the house and even cuddled up to sleep together on the bed at nighttime.

WE'RE A TWOSOME!

Poggles and Tatenda have grown too big for the ranch so they now roam the parkland instead. They can meet their own kind but still stick close to each other as well.

WATER BUDDIES
Here, German photographer Nadine Umbscheiden snorkels up close to a swimming pig. She proved so popular with the underwater porkers that she was named the "pig whisperer."

"You never know what you'll see when you're out tracking down wildlife."

Photographer Eric Cheng, who snapped Nadine and her piggy swimming buddy while on a diving expedition

Life's a Swine

When relaxing on a beach vacation, the last thing you would expect is to have to share the water with a pig. But you'd better think again if you're heading off to Major Spot in the Bahamas. Turning up their snouts at barnyard mud, here a group of roaming porkers enjoy trotting across the sands and taking a cool dip alongside us humans. As well as splashing about, these beach bums swim out to greet-and-squeal at any incoming boats. So common a sight are the brown and pink hogs that their favorite hot spot has been renamed Pig Beach. With that sizzling sun, we wonder if Bacon Beach might be more appropriate. Or are we just being rash-er?

PORKIE PICKINGS
Cast your eyes over these piggy facts.

• Pigs have an exceptional sense of smell and can even sniff out food from under the ground. That's why their snouts are always buried in the dirt.

• A pig can swig down up to 14 gallons/ 64 liters of fresh water a day.

• A pig's sweat glands don't work. That's why it rolls in mud to keep cool.

• The squeal of a pig can be louder than the noise of a jumbo jet taking off!

Fido Fitness Camp

The dogs in Colombia are spoiled rotten! Not only do they have the finest weather to bask in but some owners will pay up to $106 a month for their cushy canines to be bused to a doggie day camp center for fun and frolics. As well as woofing their way through workouts, the dogs do exciting stuff like swimming, ball chasing, and other games. It sure beats regular walks. But spare a thought for the poor bus driver who, at the end of the day, has to chauffeur the pooped pooches all the way back home ... for 19 miles/30.5 km. What a grueling and drooling nightmare!

Mad Max

You wouldn't want to find yourself getting into a scrum with this rugby-loving muscular mutt. Max is a 14-month-old Boxer dog who is an honorary member of the Whitecraigs Rugby Club in Scotland. His favorite pastime is running onto the pitch and going for a try. We recommend though that the ref never argue with him over a penalty.

Dog That Dared

You might just be looking at the world's most incredible dog. Peer closely at the picture and you'll see that Dare, a Shetland sheepdog, has only two legs. Yet that doesn't stop him from leading a full and exciting life. In addition, Dare has proved to be an inspiration to us humans. With his owner Tami, he regularly visits seriously ill folk as part of an animal therapy team. People always feel a whole lot better after spending some time with this plucky pooch.

Some Like It Otter!

You can now add a new sort of lolly to your summer thirst-quenching favorites – fish-flavored! Don't worry, though, you don't have eat it, because this bizarre bar of ice was invented for overheating and undereating otters at the Blue Reef Aquarium in Portsmouth, United Kingdom. Asian otters Patty, Selma, and Ralph loved their lollies so much that they even learned to hold on to the wooden sticks themselves!

OTTER LOLLY – THE RECIPE

1 glass of water
4 small chunks of trout
5 grapes
1 carrot, chopped
1 banana, chopped

Stir the treats into a cardboard cup of water, to make a fiendishly fishy concoction. Pop in a wooden stick and freeze. Once ready, er ... find an otter and give it the lolly. Good luck!

Cat's a Nice Mess You Made

Don't get us wrong, we love cats, but really, when they're kept indoors, there's always that smell. You know the one – wafting out of the cat litter tray. So why can't all felines be like Doogal? He was taught to poop in the toilet by his Australian owner Jo Lapidge, who was inspired by the cat Mr. Jinks in the hit movie *Meet the Parents*. So impressed was Jo by how quickly Doogal learned to poop in the toilet that she created the Litter-Kwitter, a system that helps you train your cat to do its business like humans. That was five years ago and the product is now selling all over the world. So for your nose's sake, start teaching your cats!

SECRET PONG

Ever wondered why your cat tries to bury its poop? It's a throwback to when cats lived out in the wild. By covering up their poop, cats could hide the unpleasant smell from predators and stay safe.

Wom-boy

In rare cases, animals not only behave like us but actually want to be us! Take this adorable white wombat Stuart Little, who shares his name with the mouse from the hit Disney film. He is part of a real human family, the Mattingleys, who live in Australia. With his "dad," Reg Mattingley, he goes for walks, chats, and makes sure all the animals kept at the family's wildlife center are okay. Then after a long day, he likes nothing more than to curl up with Reg and watch rugby on television.

Clever Meerkats

No one likes the cold, so imagine how meerkats must feel in a biting breeze – they're more used to the stinging heat of South Africa, Angola, and Namibia. So when the meerkats at Taronga Zoo in Sydney, Australia, found themselves feeling the chill, they decided to take full advantage of the three lamps the zookeepers had put out for them and huddled under the infrared heat. The zoo fended off mock criticism that the meerkats were being treated like superstars, politely pointing out that their Komodo dragon lizard had its own personal heated rock!

SUN ANGELS
Meerkats were called sun angels in African folklore because people believed they could fend off demons, but judging by this photo, even sun angels need warming up sometimes!

Frog-Marched Up the Aisle

It may seem strange to us, but in India, the wedding of two frogs is a very important tradition. Each year, rural folk hold this ritual to appease Barun Devata, the Hindu rain god, and to bring on rains so that farmers will enjoy fruitful crops and a generous harvest.

Up to 2,000 people attend the event as the lucky couple enjoy a colorful and vibrant wedding ceremony followed by a fancy lunch of fragrant flies and mosquitoes. The "hoppy" couple are then released into a river and head off on their honeymoon.

TIE THE KNOT
At the ceremony, the bride and groom are dressed in wedding outfits. The bride is presented with gifts and songs to celebrate the union of these two amphibian lovers.

A Monkey of Many Talents

Back in the early 1980s, if you were passing through Lincoln County in Mississippi, you might have had to double-check when you saw Cedo. This clever chimp was often spotted plowing a field on a tractor, feeding hay to cattle or even out paddling a boat before kicking back with a fishing rod to catch supper.

At the end of a long day, Cedo would head off in his owner's truck to get beers for them both. Once his whistle was whetted and he'd eaten his supper using a knife and fork, Cedo would then take off his overalls and go to bed for a well-deserved night's sleep.

STAR ENTRY

"I am afraid somebody driving by the house is going to run off in the pond one day when they see him cutting the lawn."

Farmer Linsber Brister in an interview about Cedo to the Lakeland Ledger newspaper

CHAPTER 3
Clever Creatures

Think you're the smartest thing on two legs? Or on any number of legs for that matter? Well, you'll probably want to reconsider after being surprised by the brains and creativity of the creatures featured on the following pages.

Look out for...

MUSICAL WALRUS

PAINTING ELEPHANTS

MEERKAT SHOPKEEPER

Champion Chimp

So where do we start with Louie the chimpanzee's amazing list of achievements? Well, obviously he can skateboard, but he can also heel-edge a snowboard and he's delighted more than a million ice hockey fans with his perfect puck handling skills. Sound impossible? If you don't believe us, you can watch Louie's extraordinary talents in the MVP: Most Vertical Primate Hollywood sports movie series. What's next for this chimp? Louie the astronaut? Don't rule it out!

TOO TALENTED

When Louie snowboarded in one of his movies, he did it so well that producers had to bring in a second chimp to shoot the scenes where he was meant to be learning the sport!

Rooks Rip Up Rules

Scientists were in awe when a bunch of bright rooks showed they could use and even make tools to get food. Check out the things they did.

The rooks broke a platform with a stone so they could fish the food out from underneath it. They dropped pebbles into a tube containing a worm and a little water – each pebble raised the level of the water so, in the end, they could reach in and grab the tasty squiggling snack. They even used a hook to grapple a piece of food out of a tube. This was all the more impressive because the rooks actually made the hook in the first place by bending a straight piece of wire!

"The finding is remarkable because rooks do not appear to use tools in the wild, yet they rival habitual tool users such as chimpanzees when tested in captivity."

Appropriately named researcher Chris Bird, on the rooks' remarkable intelligence

Mystic Moggy

It may have boasted 50 rooms of the finest Victorian features but the Australian mansion known as The Abbey had a slight problem – it was overrun by ghosts! No worries, though, if you had a ghost-hunting cat called Merlin.

According to the folk who sold the property in 2009, their poltergeist-pouncing pussy could sense when something not-of-this-world entered a room. If his hackles went up, you needed to ready yourself for a spectral scare, including doors banging open and shut by themselves, dark figures sliding through the air, and a "lady in white" who gave you a scare as she stalked the stately home.

Ape-titude Test

This primate obviously means serious monkey business as he crams to learn biology in time for his exams. In the wild, these amazing apes are better known for being the best at jumping and climbing, but this swot of a Bolivian squirrel monkey lives at the ZSL London Zoo. He obviously wants to be the best in his class as well as at the top of his tree, so he certainly doesn't have time for ape-ing around!

It's mine ... no, it's mine!

Doggie Detectives

Cigarette smoking is a dog-awful habit, and these two Labradors, Clop and Chic, are determined to stub it out once and for all. They are trained and used by French authorities to sniff out illegally imported tobacco with their finely-tuned sense of smell.

Such doggie detectives are vital to law enforcement agencies all over the world. They can pick out a scent from dozens of others at a crime scene, and their incredible sense of smell is thought to be one thousand times more sensitive than our own.

WHAT A SMELL!

Dogs can be trained to find many different things, including explosives, drugs, and even mobile phones. It takes three months of intensive training for a canine to become a detector dog.

Swap Tusk for Brush

Can you believe it? A group of creative elephants at a Thai camp have made it into the record books for their incredible impressionist painting skills!

After a tough life working in the forestry industry in Thailand, elephants retire to various camps all over the country. The Maesa Elephant Camp teaches its senior citizen elephants to get in touch with their artistic side by training them how to play musical instruments and how to put a paintbrush to canvas.

RECORD BRUSHERS
In 2005, eight elephants painted a huge nature scene. It sold for $44,523 and entered the record books as the most expensive elephant painting ever.

Pixie Perfect

She looks like any other adorable puppy, but Pixie the little Border Collie is special. She is deaf and learning sign language from her trainer, Liz Grewal. Pixie is very young so she has learned only three commands so far – sit, down, and come. Research has shown that a dog can learn up to 165 signs. Some super-smart pups can even recognize up to an astonishing 250 different symbols.

SUPER SIGN
Here, trainer Liz is giving little Pixie the command for "sit." Liz has been training deaf dogs for six years now.

"They train quicker than a hearing dog, as there are no noise distractions."

Liz Grewal on the benefits of training deaf dogs

Park and Bark

Cute little dog Pipi is not just man's best friend but an entire family's. He helps out by heading to the vegetable market in Zhengzhou, China, most days, pulling a refitted children's car behind him.

Trotting along a 0.6 mile/1 km road to stock up the family's greens, Pipi is more than happy to pull the hoard all the way back too. In between his supermarket shopping trips, he enjoys giving the family's young children a lift. Yep, he's definitely the perfect canine cabbie!

Walrus Chorus

Never mind clapping flippers or jumping through hoops; that's soooo last century. Sara the walrus is quite clearly bored by such clichéd behavior and instead prefers catching a rose in her mouth, dancing the tango, or blasting out notes on her saxophone.

Sara is the star attraction at Dolphinarium, a sea life center opened in Istanbul, Turkey. We're sure she left the dolphins feeling a little miffed at her sea scene-stealing antics. But never mind, Sara can always play them a deep blues C on her sax to really make them feel miserable!

This tune's note perfect!

STILL IN LUCK
We are very lucky to see the likes of Sara. In the 1930s, walruses were on the verge of extinction due to hunting. Thankfully today, conservation programs are helping to increase the numbers of these amazing creatures.

Dog Done Reading

Willow the wonder dog is one seriously multi-talented mutt. She can sneeze on demand, has befriended guinea pigs and rabbits as playmates, and travels the world. Oh, and she has learned to read in just six weeks!

When a word is held up, either handwritten or printed out from a computer, Willow will react. Show her "bang" and she'll play dead. Show her "wave" and she'll lift her paw in the air, and as you can see in the photo, show her "sit up" and she will get on her hind legs and pretend to beg.

WILLOW WONDERS

• Willow was taught to read after a bet. Her owner Lyssa won the bet along with an all-expenses-paid vacation to Mexico.

• Lyssa and her hubby's wedding certificate features an all important second signature – Willow's inky pawprint.

The Ape Escapes

How's this for a nearly great escape? Karta, an enormous 27-year-old orangutan, managed to confound keepers and the public alike when she made a break for freedom at Adelaide Zoo in Australia. The first part of her plan saw the mischievous monkey using a stick to short out the electric wires that surround her compound. Once she'd climbed over the fence, she was confronted with another wall. Determined to continue, she set about piling up objects at the foot of the wall to give her a lift up. Karta made it to the top, only to stop and hang about for 30 minutes, considering her options. Eventually, she decided that she'd rather stay and dropped back into the zoo. Perhaps she was just proving that you can't keep a good monkey down!

Groundhog Has His Day

Each year at Gobbler's Knob in Punxsutawney, Pennsylvania, the world-famous groundhog Punxsutawney Phil forecasts the weather. On February 2, he leaves his burrow in front of hundreds of people. If he sees his own shadow, citizens can expect another six weeks of winter weather. If he doesn't, then it means spring is coming early. How does Phil communicate his prediction? Well, this crafty creature talks an ancient language known as "groundhogese." The only human who can understand him is the president of the Groundhog Club pictured here.

THE VERDICT

After conferring with Punxsutawney Phil, the president of the Groundhog Club reveals the weather prediction to the crowd. It is said that Phil is rarely wrong!

Poser Penguins

Not all wild animals flee or freeze in fear when confronted by humans. These plucky emperor penguins were puzzled by photographer David Schultz when he took snaps of their rookery in Antarctica. One trio were so curious about this strange two-legged creature with no wings that when he left his camera unattended, they decided to investigate. Much to the photographer's surprise, one of the birds ended up standing behind the lens, peering through the viewfinder, while the other two went around to the front and appeared to pose for the penguin paparazzi.

PICK A PENGUIN

Other penguins at the rookery were just as curious as the three you see here. Parents nudged their chicks toward David, the photographer, wanting their little ones to say hello to him!

Team Pigeon

Pigeons may have been labeled as "flying rats," but they can't be accused of being birdbrained. The three pictured here definitely had the last laugh on a scorching day. When the coast was clear, the first bird landed on the lever that triggers this fountain. The second swooped in to drink and bathe in the cooling water while the third kept an eye out for us interfering humans. Then they all swapped positions so each bird could quench their thirst in turn. What a bunch of clever coo-ties!

PIGEON BRAINS

Pigeons are smarter than we think. Here are just a few of their skills.

- Experiments have shown that pigeons can recognize every letter in the alphabet.
- Pigeons can tell the difference between two people in a photograph.
- They're the only birds able to recognize themselves in a mirror.

SHUT UP SHOP
When Clyde isn't working in the pet shop, he likes to snack on the supplies, including mealworms and his favorite delicacy, crickets!

Not a Mere-kat

Having a meerkat as a pet is extraordinary enough but now imagine having one as a shop employee! Clyde the meerkat has a job at his owner's pet shop near Plymouth, England. Whether he is working the till or checking on pet supplies, he doesn't mind getting his paws dirty helping out. Clyde has been hand-reared by the Wakeham family since he was a baby, so he isn't like other meerkats, who don't normally go anywhere near humans. Instead this little furry beast is happiest chattering with shoppers and hanging out with his human family.

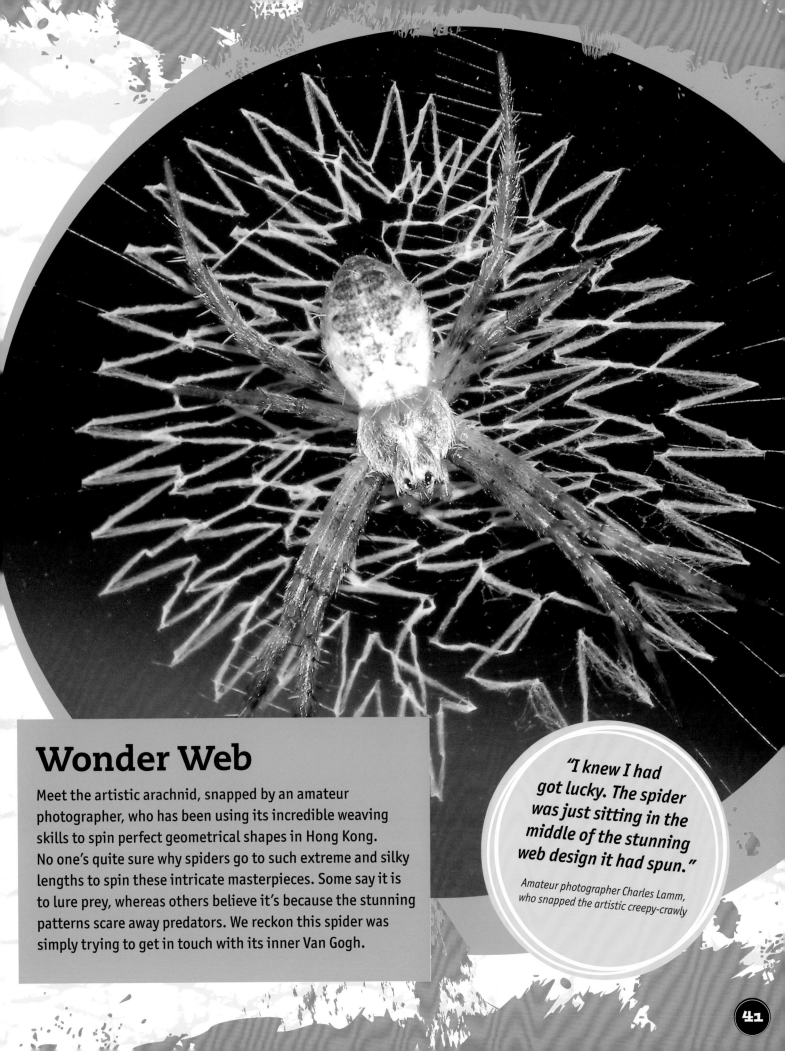

Wonder Web

Meet the artistic arachnid, snapped by an amateur photographer, who has been using its incredible weaving skills to spin perfect geometrical shapes in Hong Kong. No one's quite sure why spiders go to such extreme and silky lengths to spin these intricate masterpieces. Some say it is to lure prey, whereas others believe it's because the stunning patterns scare away predators. We reckon this spider was simply trying to get in touch with its inner Van Gogh.

"I knew I had got lucky. The spider was just sitting in the middle of the stunning web design it had spun."

Amateur photographer Charles Lamm, who snapped the artistic creepy-crawly

CHAPTER 4
Pet Pastimes

Animals are just like us. Fun activities keep them entertained. But the creatures in this chapter go way beyond going for walks or playing a quick game of fetch. These pets are real serious about their pastimes!

Look out for...

BASKETBALL PARROT

GOLFING CHIMP

TRAMPOLINING PIG

Trunk Wash Stop

If you've ever wanted to experience an elephant close up while your car gets a wax, then we recommend you visit the Wildlife Animal Park in Oregon. Here, they use their resident African elephants, Alice, Tiki, and George, to wash down visitor cars as one of the wildlife attractions.

Hand over $20, then roll up your window quickly, as the clever creatures suck up water and blast it all over your vehicle. Once the spraying is done, the elephants finish off by giving the car a good sponge-down. But don't expect a spotless job. The animals aren't known for their professionalism!

"Part of our job is teaching them new things [and] not to let them get bored."

Full-time safari park trainer Dinah Wilson explains why the elephants have been employed to wash visitors' cars

Hole in One

Meet the biggest swinger in town! This is Rudi, a seven-year-old female chimpanzee who is queen of the golf clubs. Rudi first revealed her sporting talent at the Everland Amusement Park in Yongin, South Korea, pulling in huge crowds as she putted the ball. If that wasn't enough, she went on to become an Internet sensation, attracting thousands of hits. This clever chimp has scored a hole in one with audiences and certainly doesn't need any tips from the professionals!

SLIMING ALONG

The 2009 World Snail Race Championship was won by Terri. She slimed her way through the course in 2 minutes and 49 seconds with 187 other snail competitors challenging her!

Race at a Snail's Pace

On your marks ... get set ... go. Now put the kettle on, brew a cup of tea, and eat a cookie. Yes, welcome to the slow speed thrills of snail racing. This wacky event takes place in Norfolk, England, where up to 200 snails slug it out in the World Snail Racing Championships. Audiences watch in awe as the pocket rockets dash—well, dawdle—down the 13 in/33 cm course to win a trophy tankard filled with lettuce leaves. Now, you might think that this is some crazy one-time event dreamed up after a group of adults consumed far too much alcohol. But no. The WSRC has been shelling out prizes for over 25 years and attracts thousands of spectators from all over the world.

What a Fashion Fright

It's the hairpieces that pet owners have been wigging out over. We couldn't possibly comment on how the pets feel about such peroxide locks, but sisters Jenny and Crissy Slaughter dreamed up the idea of wigs for animals after being inspired by the crowd reaction to their entries at the largest doggie festival in the U.S., Santa Barbara's Big Dog parade. Jenny and Crissy have been dressing up dogs since they were children – we can only imagine how put out their Ken and Barbie dolls must have felt!

HAIRY HAIRDOS

Flushed by success, the Slaughter sisters have created eight wigs for wacky pet owners including these four:

- "Arfro" – yes, you've guessed it, a 1970s-style Afro wig.

- "Animullet" – the classic short-on-the-top-and-long-on-the-bottom look.

- "Spike" – sported by the hair-raising green-wigged dog above.

- "Bobcat" – your cat's answer to long, luscious locks (take a look left).

WIG-AHOLIC

It's not just Americans who love these mad mops. The wigs are sold in over seven countries. So if you want to traumatize your pet with a toupee, you have 80 stores worldwide to choose from!

> "We came up with our own creative design for dog wigs that turned out so cute, people wanted to buy them."
>
> *Crissy Slaughter explains how she got hooked on making wigs for pets*

WATERSPORT WONDERS

Whether they're surfing, scuba diving, or kneeboarding (that's kneeling on a surfboard while being towed by a boat), these animals love to fool around on, in, and under the water.

One Dog and His Board

Star the torpedo terrier never whines about being bored because he's always on his board! This dog with a big sense of adventure has become addicted to kneeboarding thanks to his Aussie owner, Peter Dwyer. You can find the odd couple bombing up and down the Murrumbidgee River in New South Wales, Australia, most weekends. Star either rips along with Peter or goes solo to the astonishment of watersports fans. But don't fret about this mutt's safety. He has his own customized life jacket.

Scuba Dooby Doo

It's an impressive feat for a human, never mind a canine – 200 dives at depths of up to 12 ft/3.6 m. Yes, Shadow the Labrador is a full-blown scuba diver! When her owners Dwane and Violet Folsom used to go diving, the water-loving woof would always leap in after them and try to follow their bubbles. Convinced that his dog wanted to join them, Dwane set about constructing scuba gear for Shadow. With a special helmet that fed oxygen from Dwane's air tank, Shadow took to the water like a dogfish. Shadow is such an accomplished diver now that she has swum with stingrays off the Cayman Islands in the Caribbean.

Cat-ching the Waves

This pussy is no wussy when it comes to the waves. Peruvian cat Nicolasa has taken to surfing with her owner, Domingo Pianezzi. He discovered the four-month-old feline was fine with water when she leaped onto his surfboard as he headed out to catch a "tube" – that's a giant rolling wave to you non-surfers.

She has some style, too, according to Domingo, who also encourages his dogs to surf. He is so convinced of her talent that he plans to enter Nicolasa into international festivals to see if she can wipe out the competition!

Surf's up, kitty!

Dive, Doggie, Dive!

The Australians are well known for their outstanding Olympic swimming team, and judging from the antics of Max, the yellow Labrador, they could just have found themselves a new diver to add to their elite group for the Olympics in 2012.

Max is obsessed with throwing herself in the deep end. Her owners lob tennis balls into their garden pool so Max can dive in and retrieve them. While she always has a whale of a time, we suspect they may have developed tennis elbow by now.

TOP TECHNIQUE

It's Max-imum attack when Labrador Max launches herself into the pool. We're sure that the Olympic judges would award her five out of five for ability, style, and dedication!

Not So Daffy Ducks

Why go to all the trouble of learning to paddle in water when you can hitch a ride? These crafty ducklings were spotted on a piece of driftwood in a pond at Tymon Park in Ireland. When the beaky birds saw their mom wasn't looking, one of them hopped on, followed quickly by the other four. Then they proceeded to take a quick nap. However, mother duck quickly caught wind of their cunning ruse to get out of learning to swim and winged it over, tipping them off their perch with her beak.

> "I've photographed a lot of birdlife in the area and I've never seen ducklings as lazy as these before."
>
> Photographer Paul Hughes, who took this fantastic wildlife snap

Tusk-pin Bowling

Here's an animal that likes to strike out on her own. Moja the eight-year-old African elephant helps to raise money for conservation at the Miami Metrozoo, by regularly bowling over spectators with her spectacular ball control. Using her trunk or her feet, Moja is able to launch the balls at the pins and tries to go for that perfect game – 12 strikes in a row. Failing that, she's more than happy spending her time playing softball or football instead.

MRS. MUSCLE
Moja's trunk is perfect for throwing a bowling ball. It has up to 150,000 muscles to help her grasp.

Panda Car

Of course you would let a 17-year-old behind the wheel of a car – after all, we all want to learn to drive at that age. So the owners of Yingying, a 17-year-old giant panda, had no worries about sending him off with his own set of wheels at an arts festival in Beijing, China. Driving a battery-operated car, Yingying delighted audiences as he raced around the court, beeping his horn. In between tooting and powersliding, this gifted bear is thought to be the only one of his kind who can lift weights, slam-dunk a basketball, and slip down a slide as well.

PRICEY PARROT

AJ's owner forked over $3,000 so the sporty parrot could have his own golf course. Along with his mini-basketball hoop, what more could he want?

What a Sport

AJ the sporting parrot is believed by many to be the world's most talented bird. He can play golf, score hoops in basketball, and even do gymnastic routines. His amazing tricks include flipping around his owner's finger and giving people handshakes using his claw!

The Indian ringneck parakeet's routine has become a massive hit on YouTube. Here you can see how dedicated AJ is to his sports – to get himself ready to slam-dunk a basketball, he'll call out over and over again, "Put the ball in the basket." Talk about being in the zone, man!

Flying Pig

Mud is not enough for Scarlet the wooly Hungarian mangalitza pig. No, this little porker prefers bouncing up and down on the family trampoline. Living on the Howell family's farm in Shropshire, England, she hogs the trampoline so much that the Howell children hardly ever get the chance to play on it!

Scarlet's owners believe that she inherited her crazy jumping skills from her dad, Percy the pig, who used to love bouncing about on the trampoline, too. Alas, Percy's belly is now far too porky for him to use the equipment in case he damages it!

BOING, BOING!

Scarlet is so skillful at trampolining that her owners have entered her into the United Kingdom's premier TV talent show, *Britain's Got Talent*. What a star!

Horseplay

It's a tough life being a horse in the army. To help the animals unwind, the King's Troop Royal Horse Artillery are treated to visits to the seaside town of Blackpool, England, where they go swimming in the freezing-cold sea. The water-loving mares make a popular sight along with the donkeys on the beach. If the horses get hungry they can always swap their carrots for a stick of Blackpool's world-famous candy!

Parachutin' Pooches

It seems that canines like nothing more than throwing themselves out of planes while strapped to their skydiving owners. The world's first skydiving dog was Katie, the Jack Russell terrier (pictured above) who leaped from a plane and skydived 12,000 ft/3,600 m back in 1987.

It was an achievement not to be sniffed at unless you were a miniature dachshund called Brutus. This daredevil pooch leaped to fame when he skydived a whopping 15,000 ft/4,500 m in California, 10 years later. He fell into the world record books for being the world's highest skydiving dog.

HIGH FLYERS
Check out these parachuting pooch facts.

• Leaping dog Brutus is no one-shot wonder. He has made over 50 jumps.

• An Australian hound called Hooch is thought to be the world's first skydiving dog. She made 53 jumps.

• Hooch had to retire when she fell out of her doggie bed and broke a leg!

CRAZY FREE-FALLERS
It's not only skydivers, like Katie the Jack Russell, who plummet from great heights. One witless whippet fell 300 ft/91 m down a cliff chasing a rabbit. Luckily, it lived to tell the tale!

Dive of the Tiger

Don't worry – although this leaping tiger looks like he is about to make a big splash before enjoying a human-shaped snack, his behavior is actually encouraged by his trainers at the Out of Africa Wildlife Park in Arizona. The park's crazy keepers love to make their tigers chase them around the pool before they jump into the water, followed by the big cats. After splashing about, the tigers roar their way out, then do it all over again!

"These tigers love their keepers so they don't protract [extend] their claws when chasing or jumping into the water."

Wildlife photographer Kathleen Reeder, on why the trainers don't get clawed by the tigers

RUB ME DOWN

There are genuine massage techniques for cats. One favorite is the feline chin rub, which can help to cure cat acne. The chin is the one place a cat can't reach with its tongue.

Monkey Massage

Life's a breeze for cats in Thailand. Not only do they get to lie around all day in the scorching sun while keeping one eye open for a passing mouse, but if they live at the Chaloklum Elephant Trekking Center, they can enjoy a massage from a resident monkey.

This three-month-old pet macaque primate gave this worn-out kitty a full rubdown, and in payment he got to snack on the cat's fleas. Things nearly came to an abrupt end, though, when the monkey wanted to cuddle – the cat nipped that one in the bud quickly!

Good Enough to Eat?

Pets love being spoiled by their owners, especially on their birthdays, and now, thanks to her U.S.-based baking business, Debbie Goard has just made pleasing your favorite pet even easier. Debbie creates cakes and sweet snacks for your animals in the shape of anything you can think of. Why not feed them a sugar-coated warthog, an edible alligator, or in this case, a giraffe good enough to gobble down in one sitting? Whatever sugar-coated treat you can think of, Debbie can do it!

TOO CONVINCING!
Debbie's cakes often get mistaken for real animals. Her life-size Chihuahua cake compelled one restaurant visitor to exclaim, "Why is there a dog on the table?"

Hop Aboard

They always say that people show their best sides when there's a crisis, and it's true of animals, too, or certainly of this frog who showed his best back! In 2006, the Indian city of Lucknow was hit by a flood. Photographer Pawan Kumar captured one of the lighter moments. He spotted this accommodating amphibian offering a lift to a cheerful but bedraggled mouse. The froggy boatman whiskered the little furry rodent away to safety.

CHAPTER 5
Incredible Tales

If animals could talk, they'd tell us of incredible adventures that would make our own look positively dreary. Don't believe us? Well, settle down and be amazed by the these crazy stories from the animal kingdom!

Look out for...

METALHEAD CROC

ROCK STAR CAT

MAN KISSES LION

Monkey Rodeo

Sheep, beware! Decked out in authentic cowboy hat, shirt, and chaps, Whiplash the monkey may look cute, but when he gallops out into the rodeo on his mighty steed ... er ... Border Collie, this primate isn't monkeying around! Whiplash, the 21-year-old Capuchin monkey, is a real star. He bedazzles audiences at rodeos up to 40 times a year with his cowboy skills, rounding up sheep effortlessly.

"Whiplash is a real handful. He's very strong-willed. If he isn't fed on time in the morning, he gets mad and throws his toys."

Owner of Whiplash, Tommy Lucia, to the Denver Post newspaper

Piggyback

You won't find bacon in any sandwiches at the Cushendun Festival in Ireland – the piggies are too busy trying to be first past the finishing post. The little pigs race for the line with dolls strapped to their backs. The prize for winning? Nothing but the feeling of total triumph over the other lazy porkers.

She's got a crush on me!

And They Call It ... Puppy Love

Love can lift you up and bring you down, but imagine how heavy love can be when a 1,980 lb/900 kg horse called Leroy stomps on your head! Especially when you're only a teeny tiny Chihuahua called Berry. It looked like Leroy's and Berry's beautiful friendship was about to end. Despite taking Berry to the vet, nothing could be done, so she was brought home to die. However, Berry confounded everyone by getting up the next morning feeling perfectly fine and digging into a full breakfast. Their love lives on!

Robocroc

Here's a conundrum for you – a crocodile gets hit by car in Florida, and is left with a broken jaw, unable to eat. So what do you do? Breathe a sigh of relief because there's one less people killer lurking in the swamps? Perhaps even dance a happy jig? Shame on you! It's not crocs that have eaten 22 people in the U.S., it's alligators! In fact, American crocodiles aren't interested in us humans for lunch, although one or two of them are keen on our pets. So perhaps that explains why vets decided to perform reconstructive surgery on the powerful 10 ft/3 m male croc after his life-threatening accident.

"We barely get to enjoy our backyard. My kids won't even step out there."

Chris Marin, a U.S. homeowner, who has put his home up for sale after three of his pet poodles were eaten by crocodiles

METAL HEAD
A four-hour operation to save this croc's life resulted in two metal rods being placed along his bone-crushing jaw to the tip of his nose. His new appearance was so bizarre, doctors called him Robocroc.

A Snake's Lucky Life

Pictured here is Cambodian boy Oeun Sambat, who, instead of hanging around with his chums in the playground, prefers the company of rather large snakes. His favorite is a 16 ft/5 m female python called Chamreun, which means "Lucky" in English.

"Lucky" is probably the right name because when this king-sized snake slithered into Oeun's life, the hissy missy didn't gobble him up but became the boy's best friend instead. The locals are so amazed by this unlikely friendship that folks flock from all over the region to witness Oeun curled up with his scaly sidekick or hitching a ride on her back.

BEST FRIENDS
Ouen Sambat and his pet python have been best buddies since Ouen was just three months old.

Fear the Fish

This is no porkie pie, tall tale, or in this particular case, red herring. Rescuers found a seal pup on a U.K. beach who had been separated from her mother. She was starving. Now, we all know seals are whiskers-over-flippers in love with fresh herring but not this little pup, whom caregivers named Heidi.

When presented with the finest whole herrings, she couldn't bring herself to look at the fish because she was terrified of them. After some deliberation about how to get Heidi's official seal of approval, her caregivers hit on the ingenious idea of blending the herrings into a fish smoothie. Thanks to this clever exposure therapy, Heidi became brave enough to start feeding on whole fish two weeks later!

FISHY THERAPY
Heidi's caregivers first fed her the stinky fish smoothies through a tube. This helped her get used to the taste of fish and soon her phobia disappeared.

Paint Job

Now, this is what we call an imaginative solution. Zebra-less zoo owner Mohammed Bargouthi wanted children to know what a zebra looked like in the flesh but because of difficulties between his country, Palestine, and its neighbor Israel, it would have cost him more than $40,000 to get a real zebra across the border.

So Mohammed hit on a brilliant idea. He took two donkeys and painted on black and white stripes. They looked like the real deal ... well, at least from a distance. Thankfully, the well-meaning deception worked and the painted-up donkeys proved to be a big hit with the kids!

DO IT YOURSELF
The white donkeys were turned into zebras using a paintbrush, masking tape, and women's black hair dye!

ANIMAL ATTACK

You may have a fight on your hands, but we promise you no creatures were harmed on these pages!

Cock Crushes Canine

Pity this put-upon pooch as he tries to fend off Dudu, the one-year-old pet cock. Don't worry, though, the hassled hound wasn't hurt – he just learned not to mess with Dudu. Perhaps he should have known before, as this fighting cock has a reputation throughout the city of Zhengzhou in China for taking a very dim view of our canine friends.

Dudu stands guard by his owner's bike when he's at work, hitching a ride there and back perched on top of the handlebars. At home, all the dogs in the apartment complex know that they should never ever dare to go to the bathroom near Dudu outdoors, or they'll feel the full fury of his beak!

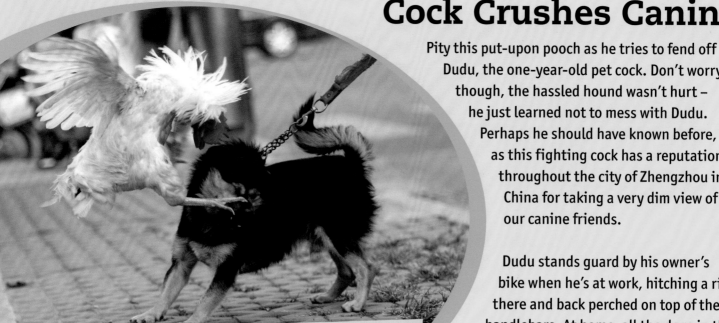

IN FOR THE PECK
The fighting cockerel has been "pecking" fights with dogs since he was four months old. Yet he has a more law-abiding side – he only crosses the road when the lights are green!

All in a Flap

Because of wintry weather and a food shortage, this normally nocturnal owl (on the right in the photo) decided to venture out during the day to see if he could catch himself a tasty snack. However, it was a desperate attempt. Each time the hapless owl managed to snare a mouse or vole, a kamikaze kestrel (on the left in the photo) would descend upon him, making him drop his lunch so he could steal it. We guess he was just none too pleased to see an owl infringing on his airspace.

OFF MY PATCH
Owls and kestrels normally leave each other well alone. Owls generally rule the night, and kestrels have it their own way during the day.

Horsin' Around

If your parents ever caught you fighting like this, they'd hit the hoof! But for these two wild stallions, who were released into the British countryside to help manage a nature reserve, sparring with each other isn't a night-mare but quite normal behavior.

Never mind such horsing around, though, these konik horses are one of Britain's rarest sights. Until this herd of 50 animals was imported into the country, their type had not been seen munching on England's green grass for over 4,000 years. It is hoped that if the horses don't end up bucking each other into early retirement, the Brits will enjoy seeing them for another 4,000 years.

LET'S GET MOWING
These konik horses help to maintain the land by grazing on the grass. That's right – they're living lawn mowers!

DINO HORSES

• The konik breed of horse is related to a prehistoric horse known as the tarpan.

• Tarpan horses roamed around Britain millions of years ago before the last Ice Age.

• They became extinct because their natural habitat was destroyed. Farmers also killed the horses for eating their crops.

• The last tarpan horse died in captivity in Russia in 1879.

"Sometimes the stallions are just playing ... but it could be a bachelor stallion challenging the dominant stallion."

Carol Laidlow, conservation-grazing warden at Wicken Fen nature reserve, United Kingdom

"The cat was much bigger than the mouse ... but he didn't seem to care. He must be the bravest field mouse in the country."

Photographer, Geoff Robinson, who witnessed the stand-off

Go on, cat ... if you dare!

Mighty Mouse

We're pretty sure this kitty was hoping that no one would ever see this picture, as it shows the cowardly cat being told off by a tiny field mouse! The perplexed pussy had dared to venture too close to the wee whiskered one's nest. Mightily unhappy, the mouse reared up on its back legs and squeaked angrily. After this prize moment was caught on camera, the cat turned tail and scampered away. We have to pity the poor puss, though, because once his fellow felines see this picture, he'll be the laughingstock of the cat world. Me-oowwwww!

Excess Baggage

Going on vacation? Sunglasses, bathing suit, sunscreen, check. Forty-four reptiles, including a carpet python – double-check! Well, that's exactly what customs discovered when they x-rayed the luggage of a man flying out of Sydney, Australia. The full haul included 24 shingleback lizards, 16 blue tongue lizards, 3 black-headed pythons and 1 albino carpet python. Thankfully, all the scaly critters were rescued while the creepy smuggler was sent to jail.

WHAT'S IN MY PANTS?
Some animal smugglers can be dim. U.S. citizen Robert Cusack was given 57 days in jail after exclaiming, "I've got monkeys in my pants!" Indeed he did.

Farmer Christmas

It might be a common sight if you live near Santa Claus in Lapland, but to see a reindeer out and about on the rainswept streets of Britain is highly unusual. Not for the residents of Enfield, though, because farmer Gordon Elliot is always taking his favorite reindeer Dobbey out for walks around town.

You can spot the peculiar couple in local fast food restaurants, window-shopping down the main street, or having a drink at the pub. Luckily, if they have one too many, they can always leave the keys to the sleigh behind the bar and catch the train home instead!

HO! HO! HO!
Each Christmas, Gordon takes Dobbey the reindeer to the local school to bring the kids a little Christmas cheer.

PIGEON DELIVERY
Pigeon mail could be the future of modern communications. One company now intends to use these birds regularly to deliver big computer files.

Send the Pigeon

Is it a plane? Is it Superman? No, it's actually a bird that delivers your computer files. Next time you're sitting in front of your computer enjoying high-speed access to the Internet, spare a thought for those whose broadband connection trundles along at a snail's pace.

One South African company got so tired of the time it took for large files to download that they challenged Winston, an 11-month-old carrier pigeon, to carry a 4-gigabyte memory stick 60 miles/96 km between two offices, and to do it faster than their usual broadband service. The plucky pigeon completed the trip in two hours. By the time he arrived, only 4 percent of the file had been uploaded.

STAR ENTRY

Give us a kiss!

The Mane Attraction

Known for their razor-sharp teeth that can bite through steel and paws that can break bones with a single swipe, lions are fearsome critters. Their fiery tempers terrify us humans. Well, nearly all of us! Enter Kevin Richardson, who instead of running in terror from big cats, prefers to play, swim, and even spend the night asleep with them, using their bellies as pillows.

This amazing zoologist and animal behaviorist who works in South Africa has astounded the world with the incredible bonds he has forged with not only lions but also leopards, cheetahs, and even hyenas, who have made him an honorary member of their clans.

"I have to rely on my own instincts to gauge an animal or situation ... It may be dangerous, but this is a passion for me, not a job."

Animal expert Kevin Richardson, talks to the Daily Mail newspaper about how and why he gets up close and personal with lions

LION LOSS

Kevin isn't just kissing a lion for kicks. He wants to raise awareness of their plight. Over the past decade, the lion population has dropped from about 300,000 to just 23,000.

Dr. Terrapin, MD

She may look like a cute reptile who simply wants to head off to the nearest stretch of water, but this terrapin and many others like her are considered to be blessed with magical medicinal powers in Cambodia. People flock to the local temple outside the city of Phnom Penh to have a Bhuddist monk or nun place the revered terrapin on their body in the belief that it will cure them of ailments such as rheumatism (painful joints). This particular turtle was donated to the temple by a local fisherman. We're pretty sure that he can book himself in for treatment free of charge with the amazing Dr. Terrapin any time!

ANIMAL MAGIC

Cambodia, like many Asian countries, has a long-held belief in the healing power of animals. Terrapins, cows, and snakes are all thought to have medicinal powers.

A LONG LIFE

Some people believe that owning a cat can increase your life span because it makes you happy. Cat café fans must agree, as the venues are usually fully booked!

Cat Café

Feeling uptight? Then we recommend moving to Japan, where cat therapy helps to soothe its stressed-out citizens. Walk around Tokyo and you'll discover cafés serving cappuccinos, cakes, and kitty cats to console you.

For around $9 an hour, you can stroke a purring (or yawning) cat to ease your woes. Some cafés have up to 20 cats waiting for your attention. Most are female, as male cats are notorious for fighting and marking their territory with urine. In a café, your coffee cup would be seriously at risk. Yuck!

Walking Again

You're looking at a remarkable sight – the first elephant with a fake leg. Mosha, a four-year-old Asian elephant, lost her right front leg after she stepped on a land mine. For two years, she had to make do with moving around on three legs.

Thankfully, Mosha was rescued by the Friends of the Asian Elephant Hospital in Thailand. Dr. Therdchai Jivacate, a specialist in building human artificial limbs, created a new leg for her from plastic, metal, and sawdust. The new limb was so successful that Mosha can now walk and even run. Recently, she had the leg replaced with a bigger one because she is growing so fast.

What a Baa-rgain?

This Scottish ram is one luxurious sheep. In fact, it's believed to be the world's most expensive sheep, having been sold for a staggering $354,600 in 2009. Former owner Graham Morrison said the price surpassed his wildest dreams.

Farmer Jimmy Douglas, who bought the ram, named Deveronvale Perfection, is not one for having the wool pulled over his eyes. He reckons his new addition is worth it. That's because he intends to breed from it and make his money back by selling the lambs. We're sure he'll make a mint!

RAKE IN THE CASH

Britain's formerly most expensive sheep, Tophill Joe, sold for $196,500 in 2003. He fathered lambs that together were worth more than $1.5 million.

Secret Stowaway

The feline-adoring Austin family were left frantic with worry in 2009 when one night their cat Sandi didn't return from his evening walk. Four days of searching passed before the almost heartbroken family received a phone call informing them that Sandi had been found in Spain, an incredible 720 miles/1,159 km away from the Austins' home near the seaside town of Portsmouth, England.

Authorities believed that Sandi had climbed under the hood of a car, fallen asleep inside and then been driven onto a ferry bound for Bilbao, Spain. Thankfully, he was spotted at the Spanish port by a deckhand, and then immediately taken to a local vet, who was able to trace Sandi's owners.

WHIRLWIND TRIP

Sandi's globe-trotting tour was definitely a trip of a lifetime.

- For his return journey, Sandi was given his own en suite cabin on the ferry.

- He was treated to an extravagant meal, including the finest salmon and chicken.

- Crew members visited him every hour to stroke him and make sure he was comfortable!

Taxi, Please!

Sergeant Podge enjoys driving his owner around in circles literally! Every night, this cat disappears and then is found in the same spot in the morning precisely 1.5 miles/2.4 km away, waiting for a lift home. Sergeant Podge has received this luxury chauffeur service for many months. U.K. owner Liz reckons it's because a neighbor who used to leave food out for Podge has left the area, so he may be heading off in search of new treats.

CAT-CHING A LIFT

Sergeant Podge has a car-loving rival called Nancy. This mischievous cat managed to hitch 12 rides in the space of three weeks by climbing into neighbors' cars when they weren't looking!

CROONING CATS

We all know that cats can do the most amazing things, but to form a band, make a record and then release it to adoring fans – that's heads and whiskers above the rest!

Meet the Band

You won't find these rock stars behaving badly after a sell-out gig. No, they're much more likely to be clawing frantically at curtains than throwing TVs out the window, or chasing mice rather than hanging out with fans and throwing up ... fur balls. Meet the Japanese pop sensation Musashi's, a five-cat band that has taken Japan, the land of the rising sun, by storm since they formed back in 2007.

PET PERFORMANCE

The talented five-piece band is made up of the following feline members, each with their own skills at the microphone.

- Musashi – male, lead cries
- Leo – male, quiet crying noises
- Luca – female, high-pitched crying noises
- Seri – female, main vocals
- Marble – harmonies

THEY'RE ROCKING!
Band members have their own personal musical equipment customized to size and featuring the group's name. Now, that's what we call true rock stars.

Lead Vocal Sensation

Feline frontman of the rocking cats is six-year-old Norwegian forest cat Musashi, pictured here. Along with his four pals, he has been littering the music charts with Christmas and New Year classics, including "Jingle Bells" and a Japanese version of "Auld Lang Syne" called "Hotaru no Hikari." They'll be a tough act for any ambitious feline to follow!

DOWNLOAD IT
Musashi's songs are so popular in Japan that they are now available to download onto mobile phones and computers.

Musashi gets ready for a rock anthem!

Contractual Cats

The fur-ball five have yet to undertake any world tours, but they do have their own management company. According to the cats' contract, the management must "pay" a skipjack tuna to each puss for every song they produce. The crooning cats have also become a worldwide Internet sensation. The band's first single, "Jingle Bells," was viewed more than a million times on YouTube and was even nominated for YouTube's Best Video of 2007 award!

一年生になったら

MUSASHI'S

CHAPTER 6
Animal Obsessed

There are owners and even entire countries who love their animals way too much. Check out this whistlestop tour of continents and people who are utterly crazy about their pets!

Look out for...

SHEEP RIDES IN CAR

FANCY-DRESS POODLE

HOTEL FOR HOUNDS

Snake Charm School

School lessons can be boring, real boring! But if you're a member of the Vadi tribe in India, we can assure you that you will never find a lesson dull. That's because this tribe has swapped sums for snakes!

Starting at the age of two, both boys and girls are taught the ancient art of snake charming. The boys learn to play the flute to win coiled cobras over, and the girls are taught to handle the scaly reptiles and make sure that they are properly cared for. Sure beats hiss-tory lessons.

> "We explain to the children how we only take a snake away from its natural habitat for seven months. Any more is disrespectful ..."
>
> Babanath Mithunath Madari, chief snake charmer

SPECIAL DIET
The cobras used in the classes can deliver a painful bite, but their poison is no longer lethal thanks to a special diet.

Canine Cuisine

Don't worry, we're not going to teach you how to cook a pooch in pepper sauce! No, featured here is merely the latest in a series of novelty shops aimed at indulging your dog. Dr. Pro in Taipei, Taiwan, is an ice cream parlor where your pooch can dig into its favorite ice cream treats.

Hungry hounds should also consider heading to Seoul in South Korea, where they can indulge in cooking classes and learn how to rustle up a quick cake ... or three. We suspect, though, that you might have problems keeping your dog from wolfing down all the ingredients before it's actually made anything!

NO PONG
In the U.S., you can now buy ice cream for dogs that improves their smelly toilet habits. The ingredients include marshmallow root, nettles, and licorice root water. Yum!

ROLL AROUND
Even many anti-bullfighting organizations are happy with these displays of dexterity because the bulls aren't hurt. Man and bull are on equal terms!

What a Load of Bull

There's much controversy surrounding bullfighting in Spain, but here's a lethal hobby that could see the bulls getting their own back. The rules are simple. You take up to three bulls and seven members of a "Recortadores," or bull-leaping team, and you place them in a ring in front of a cheering crowd.

Now watch in awe, and just a hint of horror, as the bulls thunder toward the men, who must then leap over these snorting mountains of rage to avoid being bashed to bits. Thankfully, the Recortadores are incredible acrobats and can pull off amazing jumps and flips to ensure that they live to leap another day.

Woof, Woof, Grrr ...

Knowing dogs, the above probably translates into "Food! Food! Now!" But if you're not sure and feel that your dearest doggie needs a spot of real one-on-one talk time, we recommend the remarkable Bowlingual voice device that its makers claim can actually tell you how your hound is feeling.

For it to work, you must first attach the wireless microphone to your pooch's collar. That in turn transmits the mutt's whining to a handheld console. This analyzes and "translates" what your dog is trying to tell you into one of six emotional states, which the handheld will then tell you. It's as if woofs are being turned into words!

STAR ENTRY

Bowlingual voice

TALK TO ME
The makers of the Bowlingual dog voice device reckon it has huge benefits for pet owners. This is what they say:

• It helps you to get more in touch with your dog's emotions.

• It comes with a built-in answering machine so you can catch up with your dog's news while you're away.

• It was created with the help of professional veterinarians who really know how to "talk to the animals."

LOST IN TRANSLATION
What do you think the dog is saying in this picture? We reckon it's "Can you take that ridiculous microphone off my neck!"

PAMPER YOUR PUP

Dogs are said to be our best friends. So to show how much you appreciate your four-legged friend, it's time to shower them with the very best treats.

LET'S CHAT
Pictured here is Tinkerbell, a Chihuahua-Pomeranian mix dog, seemingly having a babble with a baby!

Wheel Go for a Walk

Canine-crazed Japanese owners love their dogs so much that they treat them like human babies. If you visit one of Tokyo's parks, you'll see barking mad owners pushing their dogs around in strollers.

There are many loopy reasons why people use doggie strollers. Apparently, you can go for a jog without your poor pup becoming overexercised in the process. It's also much easier to visit restaurants with them safely buckled up, and you make your dog feel like a Very Important Pooch!

Time for a Trim

The Chinese are passionate about their pooches, too. Perhaps it's because in some cities, each household is allowed to have only a single dog. This strict rule means that the charmed canine is pretty much guaranteed to be spoiled rotten by its owners. A trip a week to the local pet salon for a full bath followed by a haircut by a professional groomer is not uncommon. It's hardly what you'd call a dog's life, eh?

Dances with Dogs

You might think it strange to do the tango with your terrier, but in Japan, dancing with your dog is positively encouraged. Not sure how to do strictly ballroom with your boogie-loving mutt? Then enroll at the Wan Nyan World dance class.

Owners and their four-legged dancing partners are encouraged to perfect their fancy detailed moves by dog-trot diva Mayumi Ozuma, who teaches the hounds to gracefully step between their owners' legs and circle them in serious salsa style. Some owners take the hobby so seriously that they even enter their doggie dancers into competitions!

"Whether it's a Chihuahua or a big St. Bernard, if you have the right music, any dog can dance. Even age doesn't matter."

Mayumi Ozuma,
dog-dancing expert

Hounded for a Hotel

If you're a caring owner who's heading off on your vacation but doesn't want to leave your canine quivering in a stranger's kennel, then check your four-legged friend into the Canis Resort, the world's first dog hotel chain. Dogs get their very own lodge with a bed and even a garden to play in day or night. Services include intensive training for your doggie and even a gate-to-gate service where your beloved pet can be waiting for you as you walk out of arrivals at the airport.

Time for a relaxing bath!

LIVE IN LUXURY
The exclusive doggie hotel boasts nine heated lodges that can accommodate up to 45 dogs. There are 20 dog-sitters to look after the dogs seven days a week.

CANIS RESORT®

Mutts at the Movies

Although you might have thought that all dogs are interested in is eating, sleeping, and sniffing each other's bottoms, it turns out that they are partial to big-screen action, too. The world's first, and we suspect only, film festival for dogs was held in that movie capital of the world, Los Angeles, in 2009.

Dogs (plus their owners if their pets had invited them) turned up to stretch out and watch an hour of short films dedicated to everything that goes woof.

MOVIE MESSAGE
There was a serious message behind the canine movie festival. It was held to raise awareness of PAWS, a U.S. charity that helps ill people to look after their pets.

PACK SURVIVAL
The kitty earthquake pack features sealed bags for keeping a small item of your clothing. Apparently, the smell reassures kitty after an earthquake.

Quaking in Their Boots

Experts recommend that if you find yourself in an earthquake, you should stay inside and wait it out. In Japan, though, this nation of animal lovers is more likely to rush to their cat or dog and dress it up in an earthquake survival kit. The pack contains special boots to protect vulnerable paws, a padded jacket, rain hat, and even a bottle of oil to rub into your pet to calm it down. There are three packs available – Basic, Lifestyle, and Ultimate. They cost up to $600 each – a small price to pay for keeping your pet safe, we reckon!

"This is not some little back garden loft; this is a state-of-the-art five-star pigeon hotel."

Mary Bartlett, co-owner of the poshest pigeon-breeding facility on the planet

Pampered Pigeons

Pigeons are serious business. Thousands of dollars are needed to breed the winged wonders into world-class racers. Their chances of becoming the best are improved greatly if they stay at the Ponderosa Stud Centre in Weymouth, England. This is an amazing £1 million complex built to cater to a professional pigeon's every whim.

Featuring state-of-the-art feeding and watering equipment with a computer-controlled breeding environment, the perfect pigeon can be raised and then bought by super-rich pigeon racing fans. While the feathered high flyers enjoy five-star treatment, owners can also relax and take a shower. They can even retreat to the luxury executive lounge to inspect their prized pigeons at their leisure.

GUESS WHAT?

Here are some birdbrained facts about the Ponderosa Stud Centre.

• Arabs love pigeon racing, so the facility recently transported more than 100 birds to the Middle East.

• The Ponderosa Stud Centre can hold up to 2,000 birds at any one time. This number rises in the new year, when pigeons like to breed.

• Co-owners Mary Bartlett and Tony Hane have been breeding racing pigeons for more than 20 years.

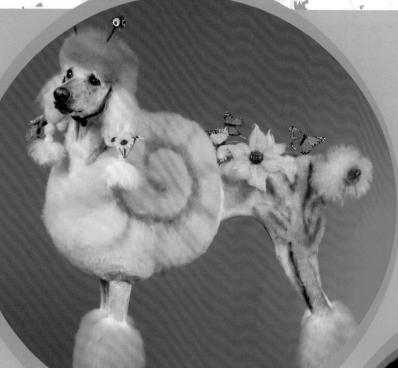

"They will go to the bathroom, they will bite you, and they will throw up. But you have to show you love and care for them through it all."

Ren Netherland on what it takes to be a great animal photographer

Posse of Poodles

You may think you're looking at a snail and ... er ... Johnny Depp, but they're all actually poodles dressed up by crazy owners who have had their dogs' pictures taken by animal photographer Ren Netherland. The poodles turn up at his amazing mobile photo studio dressed up in all manner of costumes – camels, horses, pandas, dragons, American football players and, yes, even Jack Sparrow, that scoundrel from the hit movie series *Pirates of the Caribbean*.

When Ren's not driving the length and breadth of America searching for the perfectly posed poodle, he can be found taking pictures of pets belonging to the glitterati. He's photographed Hollywood star Billy Bob Thornton's mutts and silver screen siren Kate Hudson's pets.

HIT THE ROAD
In one year, photographer Ren traveled 17,000 miles/27,359 km around the U.S. taking snapshots of costumed canines. His luxury coach doubles as a mobile studio.

House of the Lambs

Here's proof that if you give a lamb an inch, it'll take a mile – or your home in this case! Australian farmer Kath Shelton took pity on orphaned sheep that were left abandoned on the grounds of her farm from time to time, and before she knew it, she had 19 of them living inside her house and taking trips in her car.

Visitors to her house find themselves unable to make themselves comfortable because the sheep are everywhere. What's worse, they love watching TV. Thankfully, Kath has managed to toilet-train the wooly wonders so they do their business on a towel in the baa-throom.

IT'S SO CUTE!
Sheep lover Kath has really enjoyed watching her adopted sheep grow up. She says each one has its own personality. Take a look at this cutie – we're sure you'll agree!

Snap Happy

Reptile handler Tracey Sandstrom loves crocodiles. Mind you, she'd better, because this Aussie owns three of them, including one called Getcha, who measures a whopping 7.5 ft/2.3 m. Pictured here is Snappy the saltwater croc, who Tracey has had since he was only a 12 in/30 cm baby. Snappy has been leading a luxurious life. He has his own heated pool, basking lamps, and an enclosure to play in. If he ever gets bored with all that and the other crocs, he could always play with animal-mad Tracey's other pets – a selection of turtles, lizards, frogs, tarantulas, and scorpions.

SNAPPY BY NAME ...
... and by nature. Tracey wraps a special rubber band around Snappy's mouth when she's handling him because he once bit her. Alone in his enclosure, he is free to get snap happy!

Cheetah-ing Death

South African Riana Van Nieuwenhuizen shares her crowded house with a whole load of big cats! The normally fearsome predators are as domesticated as they can be. You can find them sticking their noses in the kitchen sink, rummaging through the laundry, playing cards, and snuggling up with Riana and her two (so far uneaten) dogs on her bed.

Riana used to work for the Department of Justice but realized she would rather spend her time looking after big-clawed predators. Her goal is to help the cheetah population increase. Their numbers have been dwindling in Africa. As of 2006, their total population stood at a mere 1,000.

CROWDED HOUSE

You'll find more than cheetahs at Riana's home. She lives with an incredible 11 big cats:

- four cheetahs
- two tigers
- five lions

SPECIAL FRIENDS

Perhaps cheetah-lover Riana should hook up with lion whisperer Kevin Richardson (page 64). Surely that would be a match made in heaven!

"I love them all but they're a handful."

Riana tells the Daily Mail newspaper how she feels about her pet cheetahs

Hoodie Hooches

Angel and Brick are two very cared-for canines. Their schoolgirl owners, Isabel and Jasmine Dicks, love decking them out in coats. They are so obsessed with making their pets look the part that they even alter the doggie clothes they purchase using the family's sewing machine to ensure the clothes fit perfectly. Sound a bit over the top? Not at all. Experts recommend that teeny-tiny dogs like Chihuahuas be dressed in winter to keep them warm because they have so little body fat and weigh next to nothing.

From Sidewalk to Catwalk

Fancy something extra when you have your nails done? Well, if you're in Wuhan City, China, you can take your cat along for a pedicure. Pink nails are a major fashion hit with Chinese women, and now their pet cats (and their claws) are getting in on the act too. The country has many pet beauticians, so fashion-conscious kitties can also have their hair shampooed, trimmed, and dyed in any color the owner wishes!

CLAWS OUT

We feel a bit sorry for the pet beauticians. It can't be easy applying nail polish to a cat's claws. Just one false move and ... meee-ouch!

CHAPTER 7
Crazy Critters

Prepare to meet some bizarre beasties in this final chapter. From record-breakers to creatures with freaky faces (and bottoms), you won't have seen anything like this before.

Look out for...

BIG-NOSED MONKEY

POISON PINHEAD FISH

TINY KILLER FROG

Colossal Croc

You need to be very special to stand out from the 60,000 fresh- and seawater crocodiles at the Samutprakarn Crocodile Farm and Zoo in Thailand. But that's not a problem for Chai Yai – he's officially the world's largest crocodile in captivity.

This mammoth man-eater measures an astonishing 19.6 ft/6 m in length and weighs a whopping 2,456 lbs/ 1,114 kg. To celebrate his world record, the king-sized reptile was treated to a gigantic feast of fish and chickens, all of them whole of course. Chai Yai chomped them down one after another with ease.

> "Crocodile meat is delicious – no fat, no cholesterol."
>
> Arporn Samakit, owner of a crocodile farm where some crocs are raised for food, talks about the benefits of eating crocodile meat

Who Are You Calling Creepy?

Just be thankful that giant squids are notoriously shy, live in the pitch black ocean depths and don't enjoy your nearest beach resort. These fantastically large fiends can measure over 40 ft/12 m in length and boast the largest eyes in the animal kingdom. One eyeball can have a diameter of up to 10 in/25 cm. If that's not scary enough, imagine eight thick arms and two long suckered tentacles grabbing on to you. Once a giant squid has ensnared its prey, it will drag the struggling creature into its razor-sharp beak. Eeek!

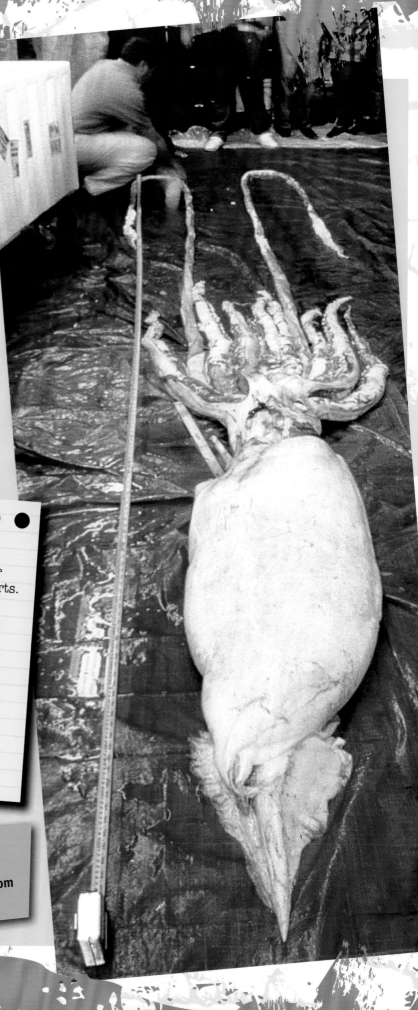

INCREDIBLE FEAT

Documenting a giant squid underwater has been a real challenge for the experts. Here's how they achieved it.

• Experts dropped a fishing line with a yummy shrimp and camera attached.

• After 20 tries, they managed to catch a giant squid by one of its tentacles.

• The squid escaped by breaking off the tentacle, but luckily hundreds of photos were taken first!

WHAT A FREAK!

The giant squid pictured here was netted off the coast of New Zealand. It measured 25 ft/7.6 m from its top to the end of its longest tentacle.

Cool Cat

This feline's feeling fine because she's been declared the world's tallest pet cat by Guinness World Records. She measures an incredible 17.1 in/43.4 cm from shoulder to toe. Going by the name of Scarlett's Magic, this whiskered wonder is a savannah cat, a mix of a serval cat (an African wild cat) and a domestic cat. Her owners, cat breeders Lee and Kimberley Draper, are proud to tell people that her famous height is no tall tale. Indeed, Scarlett's Magic has become so famous that she has already been schmoozed by stars at the MTV Awards.

"Savannahs can be walked on a leash, learn to fetch, and they enjoy the water.

U.S.-based cat breeder Kimberly Draper talks about the joys of owning a savannah cat

Show-off Spider

The things men will do to impress women – and it would appear that human males are not alone! Take this tiny spider that measures a mere 0.15 in/4 mm. When it sees a lady spider, it transforms itself from a normal arachnid into a technicolor marvel. The amazing display is made by two flaps folded down the side of the male's abdomen. The spider lifts up the flaps to reveal those incredible colors. Then it dances and shakes them all about. It's enough to make any female spider swoon, guaranteed!

SPIDERMAN
This photo was taken by Jurgen Otto, who lives in Australia. He's so obsessed with these web spinners that he's created a habitat on his dining-room table for them to play in. Ugh!

UNDERWATER WEIRDOS

We guarantee you'll be thinking twice about going into the sea after reading about this bunch. You'll either be laughing too hard to swim or too terrified to even dip your big toe in!

PERFECT DISGUISE
The leafy sea dragon's crazy looks aren't just for show. Those leafy bits make it look like seaweed and provide camouflage from predators.

Male Has Babies

While it may look like something you'd expect to find in a video game rather than in the ocean, this South Australian leafy sea dragon is not the stuff of science fiction. No, it's even weirder. The basic rule of nature in the animal world is that the females get pregnant and give birth. Not these amazing sea dragons, though. After the male and female spend the evening dancing together, the female lays its eggs under the male's tail. Then he must look after them before the wee sea dragons hatch two months later!

Stony-Faced Fish

If you're swimming off the coast of Northern Australia or paddling in the Indo-Pacific, you may want to be careful about where you put your feet down. The barnacle-encrusted rock near your foot could be a poisonous reef stonefish. This underwater terror has spines lying on its back. Step on them and they will shoot up and inject you with a deadly poison. The delightful concoction causes horrific pain, massive swelling, paralysis, and more. You need to get medical treatment immediately; otherwise you may well find yourself six feet under!

SILENT TERROR
There are 1,200 poisonous fish on this planet, and the stonefish is the most deadly of them all!

Poison Pins

Predators should be very wary of the porcupine pufferfish. It looks harmless in its normal state, but when a predator attacks, it's in for one serious shock. Firstly, this fish inflates its own body until it is a very impractical-to-eat sphere shape. Secondly, it sticks out its sharp spines. Take a look right. A predator foolish enough to try to take a mouthful can expect to be paralyzed by the poisonous pins. If you believe we humans would fare any better, then think again – eat an unprepared porcupine pufferfish, and you'll be dead within 30 minutes!

DEATHLY DELICACY

Even though they're deadly, people do eat one kind of pufferfish known as "fugu." This delicacy is prepared by specially licensed chefs who remove the lethal poison.

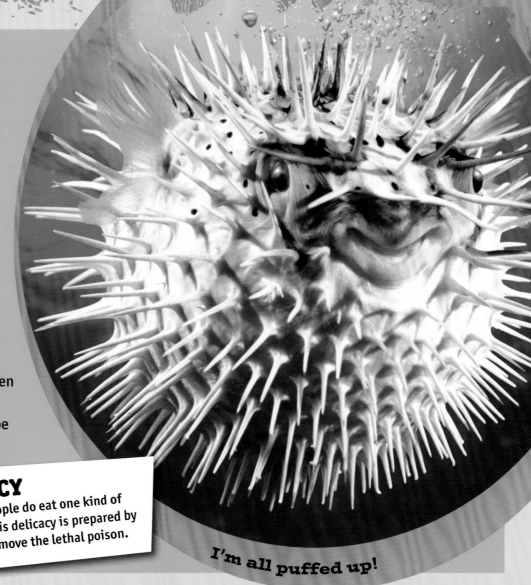

I'm all puffed up!

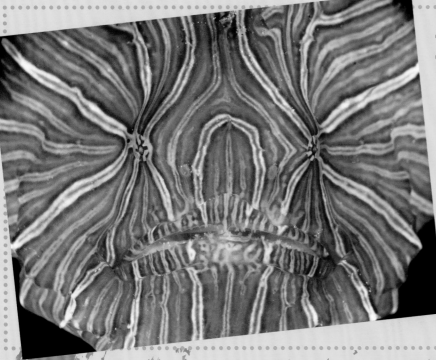

Hopping Hilarious

Meet the bonkers psychedelic frogfish, which was first spotted by speechless scuba divers in eastern Indonesian seas in 2008. This bizarre fish sports crazy colors that give it the appearance of hard coral while it bounces along the seabed like a frog! The incredible action is created by the freaky fish pushing off the seabed with its fins and using water expelled from its gills to shoot forward.

Little Bitty Bird

So little, it's sometimes mistaken for a bumblebee, the bee hummingbird is the world's smallest bird. Unofficially, it's the cutest, too. Even though tiny, its achievements are huge – it has the highest body temperature of any bird and boasts the animal kingdom's second-highest heart rate. That's not surprising, really, when you consider it can beat its wings 80 times per second. When it's showing off to a mate, the beating climbs to a staggering 200 times a second. The bird's other party trick is that it can hover almost still in the air, just like a helicopter.

Underwater Yeti

You've already met the legendary hairy Yeti earlier in this book (page 15). Now here's an undersea version, living about 1.5 miles/2.4 km below the surface of the South Pacific Ocean.

This is a yeti crab, so called because of the hairlike fibers that grow on its legs and arms. It was first discovered in 2005 and had to have a whole new sub-family of animals created for it. No one is sure what those hairy fronds do, but some people suspect that they catch bacteria, which the crab then feeds on. Whatever it is, we're glad the crab is all the way down there under the water and not in our backyards!

MAGIC MIRRORS
Hummingbird feathers are like tiny mirrors, changing color depending on where they are in relation to the sun. Pluck one out and you'll see almost no color at all.

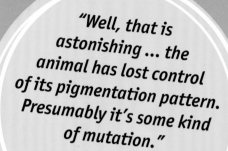

"Well, that is astonishing ... the animal has lost control of its pigmentation pattern. Presumably it's some kind of mutation."

Dr. Allan Baker, a bird scientist, talks to National Geographic magazine

Where's My Tuxedo?

One in a zillion – that's what experts are calling this amazing all-black penguin spotted in Antarctica. Penguins are famous for their black "tuxedo" jackets and white "shirts," but an all-black penguin has never been seen before. Now, you might be worrying that this fella's unique looks will make other penguins steer well clear, but fret not. The *National Geographic* journalist who photographed the black bird believes this fish-loving fella has a mate!

Eight-Legged Freak

Look who's dropped in for dinner – it's a goliath pinktoe tarantula taking a stroll across the face of its owner, Cody Wil, in San Francisco. This species of spider is in fact the biggest in the world and, for our money, the scariest-looking arachnid. Although these spiders do have venom, you shouldn't worry too much about being bitten by one of them. At best, it will be a dry bite that contains no poison, and at worst, the poison will simply cause a little pain. However, we suspect that the biggest and most serious threat if you're assaulted by one of these huge creepy-crawlies is a fright-induced heart attack!

RECORD-BREAKING PET
The world's biggest pet spider is a goliath bird-eating spider called Rosie. Her body is 4.7 in/12 cm long and her leg span is an incredible 10.2 in/26 cm.

Popular Pooch

Can you believe it? This dog is more popular than Hollywood superstar Brad Pitt. When George, the world's tallest dog, appeared on the Oprah Winfrey talk show, staff said they were more excited about meeting the truly Great Dane than the actor superstar. Now you can see him, you may understand why – this vertically challenging hound measures 43 in/109 cm from paw to shoulder and 7.2 ft/2.2 m from nose to tail.

The four-year-old Great Dane is so huge that he has his own queen-sized bed to stretch out on, and if he stands next to a sink, he has to lower his head to reach into it. You don't want George to accidentally step on you either. He weighs a colossal 245 lbs/111 kg and his paw is as big as his U.S. owner Dave Nassar's hand.

MOVE OVER
Giant hound George is so large that he needs three seats to himself on a plane when he goes on vacation!

"In my 45 years of experience of working with giant breed dogs, without question, George is the tallest and largest dog I have ever seen."

Dr. William Wallace from the Buena Pet Clinic, quoted on George's website

Big-Nosed Monkey

Now, that's what we call a hooter! Measuring up to 7 in/18 cm long, this amazing set of nostrils is found on the male proboscis monkey, which lives exclusively in Borneo, Southeast Asia. That nose isn't just there to be picked, though. Experts believe that when the male is trying to attract a female, it will inflate its nose to show off. The huge honker also helps to make angry calls louder to scare off predators. One more outstanding feature is the monkey's giant belly. This is usually stuffed full of its favorite food – leaves.

Teeny Tortoise

It's the smallest tortoise in the northern half of the world, and as you can see, it can sleep inside a matchbox. The rare Kleinmann's tortoise, which is sometimes called the Egyptian tortoise, used to be common in Egypt but is thought to be extinct there now. The cute shellsuit-sporting critter featured here was actually one of three born at ZSL London Zoo. Don't expect him to get much bigger – at full adult size, a Kleinmann's tortoise reaches a mere 4 in/10 cm.

Betty Boo

She's massive and she's got a bad attitude – meet Betty the reticulated python, who is believed to be the longest snake in Europe. Measuring in at a slithering 23.7 ft/7.23 m, Betty lives on a private snake farm run as a visitor attraction by snake lover Karsten Wöllner.

You might think that being so long means Betty can't move quickly, but she did once escape. It took five handlers and two attempts to get her back again. On the first attempt, the helpers were forced to leap out of a nearby window when she threw a huge hissy fit!

TEMPER TANTRUM

Betty is so hot-headed that photographers were banned while she was measured for her record attempt. Here you can see her on full display.

UGLY ANIMALS

It's all right that they don't understand English, so they won't be offended by the above title. Just try not to laugh at them if you ever meet them face-to-face.

WHAT'S IN A NAME?
The axolotl was given its strange name by the Aztecs. It means "water monster." They obviously thought the creature was pretty strange too!

The Real Peter Pan

This strange critter is a type of salamander called a Mexican axolotl. But what's even more amazing than its bizarre looks is the fact that it never grows up. In fact, this weirdo amphibian stays in its larval form underwater for its entire life. Looking like a tadpole with legs, the salamander is also able to regenerate any limbs it might lose along the way including legs, tails, and even bits of its brain and heart. It's a highly useful skill to have for a creature that has been known to live for well over ten years. Such eternal youth makes it the ugly-cute Peter Pan of the amphibian world.

FANTASTIC FACTS
Here are a few axolotl facts to weird out your friends.

• Those feathery-looking things on the back of the axolotl's head are its gills so it can breathe in the water.

• Axolotl can be found in only one place – Lake Xochimilco in Central Mexico.

• They are sometimes known as the Mexican walking fish even though they are not fish!

Who Are You Calling Ugly?

You may mistake them as extras from the classic kids' TV program *The Muppet Show*, but this duo of ugly ducklings are proving to be a big hit with kids in Melbourne, Australia, as they travel from school to school, helping to educate kids about treating animals with respect.

On the left is a Major Mitchell cockatoo, and his birdy buddy is a tawny frogmouth – well, you need crazy names to go with those crazy looks! But don't worry if you think these birdies might get bullied at flight school for their horribly cute looks; they grow up to be beautiful critters.

BE WARNED
The Major Mitchell cockatoo (left) may look like it wouldn't harm a fly while young but when it matures into an adult, it can become seriously aggressive.

It's a Sob Story

No wonder this bizarre aquatic animal, the blobfish, looks like he's about to blub – he's on the verge of being made extinct from his southeast Australian home because of deep-sea trawling. The unhappy marine creature keeps on getting caught in fishermen's nets as he drifts through water up to 2,950 ft/900 m deep. It's all the more depressing because if you tried to eat the poor chap, he would be totally inedible!

MR. BLOBBY
Perhaps unsurprisingly, a blobfish is mainly a jelly-like mass with few muscles. Its density is less than water, which allows it to bob along in the ocean deep.

Is It a Killer?

If you see this tiny brightly colored frog while out in a rain forest, you could be forgiven for thinking it's highly deadly. After all, it's called a poison-arrow frog. But it's not that simple – there are over 150 different types of poison-arrow frogs. Out of that lot, only a few are lethal. The deadly ones ooze a venom out of their skin containing 200 micrograms of toxin. It takes a mere two micrograms to kill a human. We advise you to play it safe and scram if you spot anything remotely colorful bouncing near your sleeping bag!

NATIVE NAME
Poison-arrow frogs got their name because native peoples used the frog's deadly secretions to poison the tips of their blow darts while out hunting.

I'VE GOT THE MUNCHIES
This incredible mole holds the official animal record for being the world's fastest eater. It takes it 120 milliseconds to identify a piece of food and munch it.

Mighty Mole

No, this isn't a publicity still from a new monster movie, it's the humble but very special star-nosed mole that lives underground in North America's wetlands. Although its nightmarish nose may look horrific, just remember it gives the mole its incredible hunting skills. The nose has 22 fleshy wiggling appendages loaded with nerve endings. They help it to feel out tiny prey as it digs tunnels with its creepy claws that act as spades.

"Each [appendage] is so densely packed with nerve endings that the mole could touch a pinhead with its nose in 600 places at once."

The BBC's brilliant U.K. naturalist Sir David Attenborough explains the magic of the star-nosed mole

Take a Look at My Butt

This world record–setting monkey is a sight to behold. You might think that it has a record for having the brightest colored butt or face, but no, it's because mandrills are in fact the world's largest monkeys! Those astonishing colorings, which feature a red-and-blue striped face and a pink-and-blue bottom, do have a purpose though. They help the male mandrill attract the attention of a lady mandrill in the mating season. During more chilled-out times, you'll find these monkeys feasting on fruit and small animals. They'll store some of the food to snack on later in their cheek pouches – that's their mouth cheeks, not their butt cheeks, we hasten to add!

GET AN EYEFUL
When a male mandrill sees a female mate that takes his fancy, the colors on his rump and face get even brighter!

STAR ENTRY

MIGHTY MANDRILLS
Check out these mighty mandrill facts.

• Mandrills have exceptionally long and sharp teeth.

• If a mandrill bares its teeth at another mandrill, it doesn't mean a fight is about to break out – it's usually a display of friendship.

• Mandrills spend most of their time on the ground but sleep up in the trees.

Index

Abominable Snowman 15
alligators 8
bee hummingbird 88
blobfish 93
buffalos 21
bull fighting 72
cats
café for 65
car-loving 67
climbing 20
earthquake protectors for 76
four-eared 17
frightened of mice 62
ghost-hunting 34
musical 68–69
pedicures for 81
surfing 47
swimming 23
tallest 85
toilet-using 29
wigs for 45
cheetahs 80
chimpanzees
farming 31
golf-playing 44
looking after baby pumas 25
skateboarding 33
chicks 10–11
cockatoos 93
cocks 60
crabs 88
crocodiles
as pets 79

huge 83
surgery on 57
dogs
bringing up piglets 24
cycling 19
dancing with 75
detectives 35
diving 47
dreadlocked 13
dressing up 78
film festivals for 76
fitness camps for 27
food for 72
friends with horses 56
hairdressers for 74
heart shapes on their coats 7
hotels for 23, 75
reading 38
rugby-playing 27
scuba-diving 46
on shopping trips 37
sign language for 36
skydiving 51
strollers for 74
surfing 46
tallest 90
two-legged 28
voice recognition for 73
wigs for 45
donkeys 59
ducks
clever 48
four-legged 10

El Chupacabra 14
elephants
artistic 36
bowling 48
car-washing 43
three-legged 66
frogfish 87
frogs
gives mouse a lift 53
poisonous 94
Groundhog Day 39
horses
crossed with zebras 12
fighting 61
friends with dogs 56
swimming 50
lambs
as pets 79
smallest 16
leafy sea dragon 86
lions 64
lizards
film and TV appearances 21
tiny 17
two-headed 9
Loch Ness monster 14
meerkats
heat-seeking 30
works in pet shop 40
mice
frightens cats 62
hitches lift on frog 53
moles 94

monkeys
big-nosed 90
clever 35
dressed for the winter 22
friends with pigeons 24
largest 95
massage 52
rodeo-riding 55
monsters, legendary 14–15
mystery creature 8
orangutans 38
otters 28
owls 60
pandas 49
parrots 49
penguins
all black 89
curious 39
pigeons
clever 40
delivers computer files 63
friends with monkeys 24
pampered 77
pigs
brought up by a dog 24
racing 56
swimming 26
tiny 13
trampolining 50
wooly 17
pufferfish 87
pumas 25
reindeer 63

rhinoceros 25
rooks 34
salamanders 92
seals
fear of fish 58
laughing 22
smuggling animals 62
snacks for pets 53
snails 44
snakes
charming 71
friends with children 58–59
longest 91
two-headed 9
spiders
artistic 41
biggest 89
colorful 85
squid 84
stonefish 86
terrapins 65
tigers
splashing 52
stripeless 11
tortoises 91
unicorns 12
walruses 37
warthogs 25
wombats 29
Yeti, The 15
zebras
crossed with horses 12
impersonated by donkeys 59

PICTURE CREDITS

3 REUTERS/Osman Orsal; 4 Dan Callister/Rex Features; 6 (bl) Barry Bland/Barcroft Media Ltd, (bc) Pennywell Farm, (br) REUTERS/Ho New; 7 REUTERS/Issei Kato; 8 (t) Barry Bland /Barcroft Media Ltd, (b) Imagine China/Barcroft Media Ltd; 9 (t) Craig Kohlruss/Landov/Press Association images, (b) National Geographic/Getty Images; 10 (t) REUTERS/ Cheryl Ravelo, (b) REUTERS/Luke MacGregor; 11 (b) Michelly Rall/Rex Features; 12 (t) REUTERS/Ho New, (b) Press Association Images/Center of Natural Sciences in Prato; 13 (t) Press Association Images/Pennywell Farm, (b) REUTERS/Ina Fassbender; 14 (t) Getty Images; 15 (t) Bettmann/Corbis, (b) Robert Clay/Alamy; 16 (t) Geoffrey Robinson/Rex Features, (b) Jeremy Durkin/Rex Features; 17 (b) Paul S. Hamilton/RAEI.org/Rex Features; 18 (bl) Barcroft Media via Getty Images, (bc) Louie Psihoyos/Science Faction/Corbis, (br) Solent News/ Rex Features; 19 REUTERS/Str Old; 20 (t) Andrew Milligan/Press Association Images, (c) Andrew Milligan/Press Association Images, (b) Andrew Milligan/Press Association Images; 21 (t) Getty Images, (b) REUTERS/Sukree Sukplang; 22 (t) Sergei Chirikov/epa/Corbis, (b) Michael Hutchinson/SplashdownDirect /Barcroft Media Ltd; 23 (t) REUTERS/STR New, (b) Incredible Features/Barcroft Media Ltd; 24 (t) Animal Press/Barcroft Media Ltd, (b) UPPA/Photoshot; 25 (t) Barry Bland/Barcroft Media Ltd, (b) Barcroft Media Ltd; 26 Barcroft Media via Getty Images; 27 (t) REUTERS/Jose Gomez, (bl) REUTERS/Jose Gomez, (cr) Tom Farmer/Rex Features; 28 (t) Rick Wilking/REUTERS/Corbis, (b) Solent News/Rex Features; 29 (t) REUTERS/Ho New, (b) Jane Ollerenshaw/Newspix/Rex Features; 30 (t) REUTERS/Will Burgess, (b) REUTERS/Rupak De Chowdhuri; 31 (t) Louie Psihoyos/Science Faction/Corbis, (b) Louie Psihoyos/Science Faction/ Corbis; 32 (bl) Bronek Kaminski/Barcroft Media Ltd, (bc) Richard Austin/Rex Features, (br) REUTERS/Osman Orsal; 33 Stewart Cook/Rex Features; 34 (t) Chris Bird/Rex Features, (b) Craig Greenhill/Newspix/Rex Features; 35 (t) Jef Moore/Jef Moore/Empics Entertainment, (b) REUTERS/Charles Platiau; 36 (t) Bronek Kaminski/Barcroft Media Ltd, (b) Nathan Edwards/Newspix/ Rex Features; 37 (t) UPPA/Photoshot, (b) REUTERS/Osman Orsal; 38 (b) Dan Callister/Rex Features; 39 REUTERS/Jason Cohn, (b) David C. Schultz/Solent News/Rex Features; 40 (t) Newspix/Rex Features, (b) Richard Austin/Rex Features; 41 Charles Lam/Rex Features; 42 (bl) Getty Images, (bc) NTI Media Ltd/Rex Features, (br) Craig Litten/Solent/Rex Features; 43 Jeffery R. Werner/IncredibleFeatures.com; 44 (t) Getty Images, (b) Geoffrey Robinson/Rex Features; 45 (t) Rex Features, (b) Rex Features; 46 (t) Getty Images, (b) Nathan Edwards/Newspix/Rex Features; 47 (t) REUTERS/Pilar Olivares, (b) James D. Morgan/Rex Features; 48 (t) Paul Hughes/Barcroft Media Ltd, (b) AAD/EMPICS Entertainment; 49 (t) REUTERS/Guang Niu, (b) Craig Litten/Solent/Rex Features; 50 (t) NTI Media Ltd/Rex Features; 51 (t) Sipa Press/Rex Features; 52 (t) Kathleen Reeder/Solent/Rex Features, (b) Ned Wiggins/Rex Features; 53 (t) Debbie Goard/ Rex Features, (b) REUTERS/Pawan Kumar; 54 (bl) Barcroft Media Ltd, (bc) Rex Features, (br) Zoom/Barcroft Media Ltd; 55 Dan Callister/Rex Features; 56 (t) REUTERS/Cathal McNaughton, (b) Craig Borrow/Newspix/Rex Features; 57 Barcroft Media Ltd; 58 (t) REUTERS/Chor Sokunthea; 59 (b) REUTERS/Mohammed Salem; 60 (t) UPPA/Photoshot, (b) John Connor Press Assocs Ltd/Rex Features; 61 Geoffrey Robinson/Rex Features; 62 (t) Geoffrey Robinson/Rex Features; 63 (t) Mark Clifford/Barcroft Media Ltd, (b) REUTERS/STR New; 64 Zoom/Barcroft Media Ltd; 65 (t) REUTERS/Chor Sokunthea, (b) Getty Images; 66 (t) Bronek Kaminski/Barcroft Media Ltd, (b) Tim Scrivener/Rex Features; 67 (b) Peter Willows/Rex Features; 68 Rex Features; 69 (t) Rex Features, (b) Rex Features; 70 (t) Tobias Hase/DPA/Press Association Images, (bc) Ren Netherland/Barcroft Media Ltd, (br) Alex Coppel/Newspix/Rex Features 71 Barcroft Media Ltd; 72 (t) REUTERS/Richard Chung, (b) Barcroft Media Ltd; 73 (t) REUTERS/Toru Hanai; 74 (t) REUTERS/Kim Kyung Hoon, (b) REUTERS/Nir Elias; 75 (t) REUTERS/Toru Hanai, (b) Tobias Hase/DPA/Press Association Images; 76 (t) Chris Lobina/Rex Features; 77 Geoff Moore/Rex Features; 78 (t) Ren Netherland/Barcroft Media Ltd, (b) Ren Netherland/ Barcroft Media Ltd; 79 (t) Alex Coppel/Newspix/Rex Features, (b) Newspix via Getty Images; 80 Barcroft Media Ltd; 81 (t) Solent News/Rex Features, (b) ChinaFotoPress/Photocome/ Press Association Images; 82 (bl) Steven Hunt/Getty Images, (bc) Press Association Images, (br) dbimages/Alamy; 83 REUTERS/Jason Reed; 84 REUTERS/STR New; 85 (t) Incredible Features/Barcroft Media Ltd, (b) Jurgen Otto/Rex Features; 86 (t) Cal Mero - www.calmerophotography.com/Getty Images, (b) Herwarth Voltgmann; 87 (t) Steven Hunt, (b) David Hall; 88 (t) A. Filis/AP/Press Association Images; 89 (t) Andrews Evans/Barcroft Media Ltd, (b) Kimberly White/REUTERS/Corbis; 90 (t) Incredible Features/Barcroft Media Ltd, (b) dbimages/Alamy; 91 (t) Adam Butler/PA Archive/Press Association Images, (b) Animal Press/Barcroft Media Ltd; 92 NHPA/Stephen Dalton; 93 (t) Alex Coppell/ Newspix/Rex Features, (b) Greenpeace/Rex Features; 94 (t) Press Association Images, (b) Rod Planck/Science Photo Library; 95 (t) Kevin Schafer/Alamy, (b) Mark Bowler/Alamy.

Disclaimer: Every effort has been made to locate the sources of the images reproduced within. Should the copyright holder wish to contact the publisher, please write to Arcturus Publishing in London.